A STUDY IN ROMANS

By the same author:

THE RELIGIOUS THOUGHT OF ST JOHN
ST MARK AND THE FOURTH GOSPEL
THE DRAMA OF THE FOURTH GOSPEL
THE SACRAMENTS IN THE FOURTH GOSPEL
THE MEANING OF SALVATION
CHRISTIANITY AND HISTORY

A STUDY IN
ROMANS

E. KENNETH LEE

LONDON

S·P·C·K

1962

First published in 1962
by S.P.C.K.
Holy Trinity Church
Marylebone Road
London N.W.1

Made and printed in Great Britain by
William Clowes and Sons, Limited, London and Beccles

To
Jessie, Peter, and my Mother,
and in Memory of
Rosemary
who, being made perfect in a short time,
fulfilled a long time,
for her soul was dear to the Lord

ACKNOWLEDGEMENT

Some biblical quotations in this book are taken
from the Revised Standard Version of the Bible,
copyrighted in 1946 and 1952, by permission of
The National Council of Churches, New York,
and Thomas Nelson and Sons, Ltd., Edinburgh.

CONTENTS

PREFACE

THE particular needs of our day have forced theologians to pass from an emphasis on a theology of explanation based upon the Incarnation to a theology of redemption based upon the Cross of Christ. This is one of the differences between the religious thought of the Fourth Gospel and that of the Epistle to the Romans. In the Fourth Gospel we find that the idea of incarnation pervades the whole of Christ's work, reaching its climax in the Cross where the glory of God was supremely revealed. In the Epistle to the Romans we see how a world frustrated and violated by sin was radically changed by Christ's sacrifice upon the Cross.

This is no doubt one reason why the Epistle to the Romans after a period of neglect in the Anglican Church is once again attracting attention. It meets the needs of a world out of joint. A theology of explanation is clearly not enough: what is required is a theology of cosmic deliverance such as is proclaimed with power in this epistle. We need, of course, both the Fourth Gospel and the Epistle to the Romans for our understanding of the Catholic faith. But it seems to me that the epistle has been neglected by Anglican theologians because its teaching at first sight appears to be too individualistic at the expense of the Church and the Sacraments. Since the Reformation the reading of the epistle has often suffered from this mistaken perspective. In fact, as we shall see, one of the main presuppositions of the epistle is the Church and that the doctrine of justification by faith cannot be understood apart from the Sacraments.

The main purpose of this book is to single out for study certain themes in the epistle and to present the argument of the Apostle in such a way as to show its relevance for the mid-twentieth century. It will be seen that much of the characteristically Jewish parts of the epistle are no necessary part of Paul's message. As we strip away what is of merely antiquarian interest we shall arrive at a message which may be applied to every age and not least our own. For example, at a time when there is much discussion regarding the relationship between clergy and laity, the epistle may be regarded as the theological charter of the layman, defining his status and dignity within the mystical body of Christ as well as his responsibilities. Paul does not concern himself with questions of hierarchy in this epistle, but with the inner mystery of the Church, its essential nature and purpose in the fulfilment of God's plan for the world.

Sometimes that which is essential and permanent in the epistle is embedded in outmoded forms of thought and expression. For this reason it has not been found possible to dispense altogether with discussions on various aspects of Jewish and Hellenistic thought. But these have been reduced to a minimum and subordinated to the main purpose which is to display the theology of the epistle as a compact unity and to draw out its permanent qualities. It is hoped that these chapters will be found useful in the preparatory work required for expository preaching on this epistle.

I acknowledge gratefully the advice given me by the Publishers and the reader to whom they referred my manuscript in its early stages.

E. K. L.

I

INTRODUCTORY

THE IMPORTANCE OF THE EPISTLE

THE importance of studying the Epistle to the Romans arises from the fact that it is the mature production of a most powerful mind. No matter how creative and buoyant a mind may be, and Paul's mind was certainly that, there is a point at which it reaches full maturity. This does not mean that it ceases to learn or to be creative when it reaches such a stage; it means that it has reached a point at which it is *formed*, so to speak, and ceases to go back on itself. If it is the kind of mind which is able to think things as a whole and to present their parts in relation to each other, there may be a moment when it may reveal itself in a very narrow compass and on what may seem a very accidental occasion. The Fourth Evangelist possessed such a mind and it will not be doubted that Paul also possessed a mind of this sort. Great man of action though he was and able to become all things to all, he never argues the smallest practical question without setting it in the light of ethical principles. It is the same in regard to doctrine. The comprehension of the Christian faith by the intelligence, the defining of its relations to all else that made up his world were necessities of existence to him. There is nothing inorganic in his intelligence, nothing that simply lies there unrelated to what has gone before or comes after. Thus Paul, less than any other author, admits of being a repository of detached texts.

CHARACTERISTICS

In the apostolic age, gospel and theology were an integrated whole. And Paul's theology is not something which anyone can separate from his gospel; it is his gospel as his mind has grasped it. The theology of Romans is undoubtedly the theology of an evangelist: it is what we might call "mission theology". The Epistle to the Romans is not a cold rational production of a patient theorist: it is the mature fruit of a great religious experience. Even so, the epistle is systematic in a sense that no other book in the New Testament is. It contains what is so rare in Scripture, and what is apparently so unnatural to the Semitic mind, a train of thought. There is a definite plan and structure, and one thing leads to another till the argument is complete.

His method may be called abstract or ideal: that is to say, he makes abstraction of the particular part of the subject with which he is dealing, and—apparently indifferent to being misunderstood—treats it in isolation; giving, perhaps, another aspect of the same subject in equal abstraction in a different place. He does not guard himself or correlate his different points of view like a modern writer. For instance, writing of the law, he mostly treats it ideally, that is, according to its governing idea of characteristic function, not as a complex historical fact. Thus, when he comes to state the principle of faith, as opposed to the principle of law,[1] he finds no difficulty in taking his illustration of faith out of the books of the law. The books of Moses are in fact *characterized* by the principle of law, but they *contain* other elements. And Paul deals with them in general simply according to their characteristic idea. Once again, he deals with the history of the development of sin, as if it represented the whole history of fallen man, in Rom. 1; and then, in Rom. 2.14–16, he gives us a glimpse of another principle which has been at work all the time, namely, the

[1] Rom. 10.6–8.

rectifying action of what we to-day would call the natural conscience. This means that we must not assume that we have the whole of Paul's point of view contained in one section. We must be prepared to look for other material sometimes in the same letter and sometimes in other letters in order to do justice to the Apostle.

The style of Romans is often that of the diatribe, that is, in the then popular form of public address, replete with crisp staccato phrases in which the writer to make his argument the clearer represents himself in a dialogue with an imaginary interlocutor. Thus it is surely not the Roman Jews whom he addresses when he writes: "but if thou bearest the name of a Jew, and restest upon the law, and gloriest in God. . . ."[1] He is simply answering the objections which opponents might logically raise to his Christian readers as they had often done to him personally in the past. This is particularly true in regard to Rom. 9—11. Thus, Paul can only be rightly understood when we keep constantly before us a clear idea of the opponents' position which he is combating as well as the purpose he had in mind when he wrote the epistle.

THE PURPOSE OF WRITING THE EPISTLE

The Christians in Rome formed a community of diverse elements drawn from various creeds and nations. There were Jews from Palestine, some of whom, like Andronicus and Junias, Paul's kinsmen and fellow prisoners, were of note among the apostles at Jerusalem, and were "in Christ" before Paul himself (16.7). There were Jews of the Dispersion, like Prisca and Aquila, Paul's chosen disciples and devoted friends. There were proselytes of Rome, now turned to Christ. There were Gentile Christians of whom some like the well-loved Epaenetus, the first fruits of Asia (16.5), had been Paul's own converts; others like Amplias, Urban, and Stachys, were his

[1] Rom. 2.17.

helpers in Christ and dear friends; others again, unknown by
face, whom yet he greets by name as "chosen in the Lord"
or "approved in Christ"; while of the great majority he only
knew that their faith was spoken of throughout the whole
world.

In such a community there must have been a great variety
of thought and practice. We know, for example, that there
were differences between one group who would not eat flesh
or drink wine (14.2–21) lest they should be defiled (v. 14),
who also observed certain days as more holy than others
(v. 5), and another group who regarded all food and all days
alike. This second group was inclined to despise the former as
superstitious, and the former condemned the latter as profane.
Lightfoot thought that the asceticism here described may have
been due to Essene influences.[1] There was, however, a Jewish
sect called the Therapeutae, whom Philo distinguished
from the Essenes,[2] which combines all the characteristics
mentioned by Paul. It is at least clear that ascetic practices
were at that time common among the Jews and it is not
unlikely that they were adopted by some Jewish Christians.
We may infer that they were few in numbers and had little
influence. Yet in the desire to abate any dissensions between the
two classes, we can see a motive for one portion of the epistle
(14—15.13) which recalls the arguments found in 1 Cor.
8.1–13.

There must also have been one outstanding problem and
that was the relation between the Jews and Greeks in one
fellowship. Frequent discussions must have taken place on
such theological problems as the apparent failure of God's
promises to the Chosen People. When we read sections 1.18—4
and 9—11 we can see that this common problem was treated
by Paul in different conciliatory ways. It could therefore have
been one purpose of the epistle to show that Jews and Gentiles

[1] J. B. Lightfoot, *Colossians* (1890), p. 169.
[2] *De Vit. Cont.* iv.

were reconciled in the one Christ.[1] But, however important this question was, it is not comprehensive enough to explain the plan of the epistle.

The main motive is probably to be found in the historical circumstances in which the epistle was written. It was part of Paul's great plan to carry the gospel to the extreme limits of the West. And his genius for organization would convince him of the importance of securing a base of operations at Rome. He had, therefore, the strongest of motives to form close relations with the Christians in the capital of the Empire, motives quite independent of the internal condition of the Church there. It was natural that he should take the opportunity of sending by Phoebe a letter containing his apostolic greetings and a general survey of the principles which had actuated all his missionary endeavours.

Associated with this motive there was probably another one. At the time of writing the letter he was anxious to vindicate himself against the calumnies of Judaizing adversaries who were assailing his character, denying his apostolic authority, and constantly hindering his work. It was in order to defend himself against these attacks that made him so anxious to go to Jerusalem in spite of many forebodings of danger (Acts 20.22,23,28; 21.11–14). These adversaries were not Jewish Christians of the ordinary type, much less were they authorized agents of the original apostles: they were bigoted and uncompromising advocates of circumcision. Paul may have thought that some of these mischief makers would stir up trouble for him at Rome, and may already have done so. This epistle, therefore, may have been prompted by the desire to win the sympathy and understanding of the Roman Christians. And the best way to do this was to set down some of the fundamental truths of the Christian faith.

[1] J. Munck thinks that such discussions would take place even if the Church at Rome was predominantly Gentile, *Paul and the Salvation of Mankind* (E.T. 1959), pp. 204 ff. It may have been the case that the Jewish minority were in danger of being crushed by the Gentile majority.

Paul was the kind of man who could in these circumstances express his whole philosophy of life in a comparatively brief document. A statement which reaches to the heart of his gospel and from which certain contemporary modes of thought and illustrations can be stripped away without damaging the main structure of his thought. The Epistle to the Romans is a mature account of the faith by which he lived and for which he suffered so much. One scholar calls it "a manifesto presenting his deepest convictions on vital points and claiming the widest publicity, to secure which the apostle strives with all his might".[1]

If this letter to the Romans can be called a "manifesto of faith" it is surprising that there is no special treatment of such matters as the Person of Christ, the Resurrection, the Church, the Eucharist, and the future Advent. This is not because Paul regarded these matters as being peripheral to his main purpose of stating the guiding principles of his missionary endeavours. He wrote his letters from within the worshipping community of the Christian Church and he does not usually discuss with any fullness matters which were generally accepted by the Church. His references to such questions were usually provoked by disputes or misunderstandings in the various churches.

Nevertheless, his whole argument is based on the assumption that these doctrines taught by him in the other epistles were accepted in their broad outline by the Christians at Rome. The central theme of the epistle is the nature and purpose of the Church. His aim is to show that all believers benefit from the promises made to Abraham, and that, by baptism they are incorporated into the People of God. It is by faith in Jesus Christ that men become the spiritual children of Abraham and heirs of the promises made to the Chosen People. God raised Jesus from the dead so that all who are baptized into his death might also share in his eternal life. Eschatological

[1] Munck, op. cit., p. 199.

motives gave urgency to what he wrote in chapters 9—11. The fulfilment of God's purposes in history is bound up with the success of his ministry to the Gentiles. Furthermore, the delay in the Parousia finds its ultimate explanation in the unbelief of Israel, which makes the missionary task more urgent. The epistle taken as a whole contains a comprehensive *apologia* for the principle of universal religion and as such is as relevant to-day as it was in the first century.

PHILOSOPHICAL AND RELIGIOUS INFLUENCES

There are those who try to rob every great thinker of his originality, and to show that his teaching is a patchwork of odds and ends taken from the opinions of others. Paul has been subjected to this kind of analysis by many scholars, and the impression that is often left upon one is that Paul's theology is not in its main features the full and free expression of a deep and wide experience, but a cunningly planned and skilfully wrought mosaic of ideas borrowed from many sources. Originality, however, does not consist in irreceptivity or unresponsiveness to the thought and life of the past or present. The original man will enrich his own personality from many sources, and the range of the influences which affect him vitally will be the measure of the reach of his attainments. But we must be careful to make a distinction between mechanical appropriation and vital assimilation. A man may know very much, and may think very little; for him the thoughts of others are like the goods on the shop shelves, which can be displayed on demand, and not like the food which is itself changed that it may nourish the body for health and strength. Another man may know far less, but what he knows has so become his own that it enables him to think more truly and wisely. This is the difference between the scholar who transmits, and the sage who transforms the thoughts of men. As we study Paul's writings we come to the conclusion that his was a mind so active in the service of an experience so intense that he did not merely borrow in order to display the thoughts of others. All that came to him from his heredity or his environment was so appropriated by his individuality that we have not said the last word needing to be said about his ideas when we have labelled it with its place of origin. We must keep this constantly in mind as we now turn to discuss the influences which have been brought to bear upon Paul's religious thought.

One important source which has moulded his theology is his religious experience, pre-Christian as well as Christian. Paul's life fell abruptly into two parts, which he himself often distinguishes as "now" and "then". Yet widely separated as they are in some ways, they are intimately related to each other, and it takes both of them to explain his theology. The pre-Christian Paul had experiences into which we must be able to enter if we would understand Paul the Christian. There is in truth no "past" in the spiritual life; what we call the past lives on in the present, and if it simply ceased to be, the present itself would be unintelligible. Unlike as Paul's pre-Christian experiences were, it was one interest which dominated his life in both stages—the interest in righteousness. Before his conversion Paul may have been a missionary for the righteousness which is according to the Law—one of those who compassed land and sea to make proselytes (Matt. 23.15). The same enthusiasm which activated his pre-Christian life was later made to serve the cause of Christ. Although there must have been a period in his life when he was contented and absolutely sincere in his zeal for the law, a deeper insight into the meaning of righteousness led to a feeling of frustration and a growing awareness of the impotence of the law to overcome sin.[1] We should beware, however, of placing too much emphasis on the psychological "explanations" of his

[1] We assume that the account in Rom. 7 is autobiographical, see page 44 below.

conversion. The ultimate explanation of an event is not given when it has been psychologically analysed. Paul's own account (Gal. 1.15–17) makes it quite clear that, in his opinion, only a divine intervention, a miracle of grace, could have achieved his conversion.[1] Furthermore, he never fully realized the nature of the contrast between a life lived under the law and a life lived "in Christ" until after his conversion. His Christian experience made crystal clear the difference between having his relation to God determined by law and having it determined by Christ. These are the fundamental experiences in relation to which everything he has to say possesses a vital significance and an abiding value for the Church. Everything that enters into his theology in a living way enters into it through its connection with these experiences. His thoughts of God and of his earlier revelation to Israel, his conception of Christ and of the experiences which constitute the Christian man, his sense of God's love, his appreciation of God's wisdom, his faith in God's providence, his hope of glory, are all rooted here. It is only when we fail to appreciate this, and treat the most organized mind of the New Testament as if it were a heap of sand, that Paul seems to be an ambiguous and baffling writer. No one who writes with his concentration and passion can really be ambiguous or hard to understand; there is but one thing he can mean, even if the attempt to utter it should sometimes miscarry, and words should appear inadequate vehicles to express his thought, and that is, something which is in harmony with the all-controlling experience through which he became the bond-slave of Jesus Christ.

It cannot be denied, however, that in using the materials provided by his experience, Paul sometimes yields to contrary impulses. Sometimes he is so possessed by the difference

---

[1] Cf. 1 Cor. 15.8–10; Col. 1.1, and other passages where Paul refers to his being "an Apostle of Jesus Christ by the will of God" must be held to have a similar emphasis. Munck, op. cit., pp. 13 f, can find no reference to any previous history in the accounts of Paul's conversion.

between the Christian and pre-Christian states, between the life under grace and the life under law, that he can only define them by contrast with each other. Christianity is all that the earlier religion was not, and is nothing that it was. It is opposed to it as life to death, as justification to condemnation, as freedom to bondage, as the abiding to the transitory glory; in a word, it is nothing less than a new creation, and the Christian is another man in another world.

But at other times the thought asserts itself, that in spite of these differences, one man has come through all the experiences with an unchanging interest, the interest in righteousness, and one God has been present in them all, working towards a gracious end which has at last been reached. It is not enough to define the stages in experience such as Paul's, or the stages in the history of religion contained in the Old and New Testaments, merely by contrast with each other. It is not enough to say that one is what the other is not, and is not what the other is. Though the contrasts may be there, they are not the whole truth; in some sense the earlier stage must be regarded as the preparation for the later; unsatisfactory as it was at the moment and unworthy as it may now appear, there must be a divine meaning in it, a purpose of God connecting it in a real and unaccidental way with that which eventually supersedes and annuls it. Of this Paul was fully conscious, and it is the explanation of the superficial inconsistencies in his treatment of the Old Testament, and of the difficulty which has been felt in understanding these from his own day to our own. On the one hand he knows that a Jew is not a Christian, the Old Testament is not the New, law is not grace—and in all these negations he is uncompromising; on the other hand, he feels that the Jew ought to be a Christian, that the New Testament, new as it is, is witnessed to by the law and the prophets, and that though law is not grace, yet if there were not law, grace itself would have no meaning. Hence the balance of his thoughts sways according as he emphasizes the essential originality of the gospel, or the essential connection between the various stages in the history of the People of God. The key to all this variation of emphasis is to be found in what Paul himself had actually lived through. He is the same man chosen of God from his mother's womb; it is the same People of God which had been chosen by him from before the foundation of the world.

Most scholars agree that the greatest influence on Paul's teaching, apart from his personal experiences, was Judaism. There is plenty of evidence to show that Paul was proud of his Jewish origin.[1] He was also pleased to recall the fact that the gospel had come first to the Jews and that they were the first to have found hope in Christ.[2] "If anyone", writes Klausner, "had suggested to Paul that he cease being a Jew, he not only would not have agreed with this, but he would not even have understood such a suggestion."[3]

There is however, some disagreement among scholars as to the type of Judaism which influenced Paul. A distinction has been drawn between Palestinian and Hellenistic Judaism, the latter being held to be more liberal than the former. Palestinian Jews spoke Aramaic, while the Jews of the Dispersion spoke Greek. Doubtless with this difference of language went also differences of thought. These differences should not, however, be exaggerated. The Jews have shown in all ages a strong tendency toward unity and solidarity of mind and purpose in religion, and especially in their devotion to the Mosaic Law. This tendency was probably not less strong in the first century of the Christian era. It is quite possible, therefore, that the distinction drawn between Palestinian or Rabbinic and Hellenistic Judaism was not so rigid as commonly supposed.

---

[1] 2 Cor. 11.21–2; Rom. 11.1; Phil. 3.4–6; cf. Acts 23.6; 22.3.
[2] Rom. 1.16; 2.9–10; Eph. 1.12.
[3] *From Jesus to Paul* (1943), p. 453; cf. G. A. Deissmann, *Paul, A Study in Social and Religious History* (1926), p. 98.

Some writers who emphasize this distinction maintain that the Judaism of the Dispersion was much more strict than that taught by the Rabbis in Jerusalem, the latter being more optimistic about man's nature and salvation, and less legalistic than sometimes imagined. This is the position taken by Montefiore in his book *Judaism and St Paul* (1914); he claims that the gloomy pessimism of Paul's doctrine of sin and its relation to the flesh is an inheritance from Hellenistic Judaism.[1] Montefiore's position is weakened by two considerations. In the first place, he precariously assumes, having very little first-century evidence to build upon, that the Rabbinical Judaism of A.D. 500 can be used as a fair description of that Palestininian outlook which existed in the time of Jesus and Paul. In the second place, his book is written upon the assumption that all the elements in the religious thought of Paul must be accounted for from some external source, a view which leaves little in the way of creativity on the part of Paul, and certainly fails to appreciate the religious experience which changed the zealous Jew into the ardent Christian.

It is probable that Paul's family belonged to a puritan type of Judaism. It was a life characterized by such high standards of personal purity and uprightness as to present a contrast with pagan life that remained with Paul all his life, increasing in him a sense of the superior nature of the religion of his fathers, and a sense of pride that his people should have been heirs to spiritual blessings and ideals so lacking among the pagan peoples. The strict manner of life and reverence for the law which were inculcated in him from his youth would be further strengthened when he became a student at Jerusalem. There his studies would be concentrated upon the Old Testament, for Rabbinic learning consisted almost wholly of the interpretation of the Scriptures, and the minute examination and

---

[1] See especially pp. 1–29. This book is subjected to a searching examination by W. D. Davies, *Paul and Rabbinic Judaism* (1948), pp. 1–16. See also the assessment made by H. J. Schoeps, *Paul* (E.T. 1961), pp. 24 ff.

definition of the requirements of the law. The Rabbi Gamaliel, in whose School Paul is said to have studied, was, it seems, a man of tolerant spirit;[1] but this spirit was not shared by his pupil from Tarsus. Nor did he share the more liberal spirit of the Greek-speaking Jews of his time. He is reported, for instance, to have been in dispute with the Hellenistic Jews in Jerusalem.[2] It is sometimes said that Paul exaggerated the Pharisaic position with respect to the legal aspect of contemporary Judaism.[3] But this, in spite of the writings of scholars like Montefiore, has not been proved. The possible reaction against liberalism, however, does suggest that Paul remained, even in his Christian days, true to his heritage, drawing from it not only inspiration and strength, but also the Jewish form of his thought and writing.[4]

The question of pagan influence upon the mind of Paul has been thoroughly investigated in recent times.[5] It is only necessary here to summarize the position so that we can get the matter into perspective. There is no evidence that Paul knew Greek philosophy as taught in the Schools, and it is extremely unlikely that a man whose spirit shrank so violently from syncretistic religion, and who was such an uncompromising monotheist, ever entertained the thought of being associated in any way with a pagan form of religion. The most that can be said is that Paul knew generally the pagan conceptions of his time and understood broadly their interpretations. We

---

[1] Acts 5.34-9.
[2] Acts 9.29.
[3] E.g. Kirsopp Lake, *Paul: His Heritage and Legacy* (1934), p. 71.
[4] Cf. W. D. Stacey, *The Pauline View of Man* (1956), pp. 11 ff.
[5] See e.g. W. R. Halliday, *The Pagan Background of Early Christianity* (1925); E. Bevan, *Hellenism and Christianity*; for the view that Christianity underwent a radical transformation when it met the pagan environment, see Foakes Jackson and Kirsopp Lake, *The Beginnings of Christianity*; see also, S. Angus, *The Mystery Religions and Christianity* (1925); Stacey, op. cit.; R. Reitzenstein, *Die hellenistischen Mysterienreligionen* (1927); R. McL. Wilson, *The Gnostic Problem* (1958).

shall, therefore, consider only briefly some of the ideas which may have influenced Paul in his teaching.

Especially prominent is the claim in some circles that the mythical conception of a dying and rising god and the mysticism associated with it, so common in Hellenistic religions, gave rise to the conception of the dying and rising again with Christ which is found in Paul. The extent to which Paul was influenced by the pagan myths depends in a large degree on what we believe Paul's view to have been concerning the death and resurrection of Christ. Clearly we have reason to believe that he did not doubt the historicity of both these events in the life of Jesus. He gave them both a redemptive and cosmic significance. Christ had come to earth for the express purpose of fulfilling God's redemptive purpose for mankind, and the Christ who had risen and become glorified bore the marks of Jesus of Nazareth, the historic person who had lived and talked with men. It has been clearly shown time and again that when all the facts relating to the so-called redeemer-gods are examined, nothing comparable to this can be discovered.[1] The myths of Adonis, Osiris, and Attis which are connected with the decay and renewal annually of vegetation, and the accounts of their death bear little resemblance to the death and resurrection of Christ. And the Mithraic cult, which is often regarded as having a greater impact upon Christianity than any other, has nothing to say about the death and resurrection of Mithras.

In much the same way it has been said that Paul's teaching about the Christian dying and rising again with Christ is of Hellenistic origin. But whatever resemblance there is here either in concept or terminology it is only on the surface. The Pauline phraseology is the expression of an intense personal faith grounded in experience. The experience of being "in Christ", or having "put on Christ", which played so large a part in his religion is strictly co-ordinated with the life of faith.

[1] See e.g. S. Cave, *The Gospel of St Paul* (1929), pp. 266–72.

The dying and rising with Christ, which symbolized the putting on of the "new man" and a putting off of the old, was a continued experience, an everyday dying to sin and an everyday rising into newness of life; and every repetition of this spiritual renewal meant a growth, an enlargement of faith, and a greater achievement of Christian freedom. Union with Christ for Paul did not mean seeking identity with Christ, as devotees of pagan cults sought identity with their gods in a mysticism which deified them. On the contrary, there is nothing whatever pantheistic about the mysticism of Paul.

There are those who believe that the Adam-Christ parallel which is prominent in this epistle and elsewhere has been influenced by the doctrine of the primal man which was widely known in the Oriental world. In the so-called Adam literature (that is the late Jewish and Jewish Christian commentaries on the creation stories in Genesis) there developed "a glorification of the first man Adam which is not explained by anything in the older religion of Israel but for which we must seek another cause".[1] This glorification proceeded side by side with the pessimistic interpretation of Adam's relation to the sin of the human race. This "cognate figure" is found by Reitzenstein, Bousset, and others, in the Iranian myth of Gayomart, the first man, the prototype of all humanity, whose death and resurrection are given both a cosmological and a soteriological significance. The figure of Gayomart, so it is claimed, had found its way into Hellenistic Judaism, there transforming the person of Adam until the latter became the primal man, prototype of humanity, and also furnishing the inspiration for the Son of Man in Daniel, and for the Messianic interpretation which the figure received in the book of Enoch. Thus the celestial Adam and the Son of Man had a common origin and gave rise to the co-ordination of Adam and Christ.[2]

There are, however, pronounced differences between this

[1] W. Manson, *Jesus the Messiah* (1943), p. 177.
[2] See C. H. Kraeling, *Anthropos and Son of Man* (1927), p. 188.

primal-man myth and the Pauline doctrine of Christ. For Paul, Christ does not pre-exist as primal-man, but rather as Son of God who existed before all creation, Christ is the heavenly man, according to Paul, in virtue of his assuming our humanity, and so becoming the first-born of that new humanity which was begun in the Church and which will be consummated in him. He is thus the prototype of humanity through his incarnation, death, and resurrection.[1] We may perhaps say that traditions known and ideas received through the religious "atmosphere" at the time may have assisted Paul in expressing what had come to him through his experience of God in Christ. But they did not in any way create his understanding of the contrasting relations between Adam and Christ.

In the same way, it is not denied that Paul used a good deal of terminology current in the pagan world, e.g. the words "mystery" and "fullness". But he was a complete master of his vocabulary. Under the influence of his Christian experience, terms were moulded and subdued and made to subserve his all-consuming purpose of expressing to Hellenistic audiences the inexhaustible content of the Christian gospel. But there is no reason to suppose that either the conceptions or terminology of the pagan religions influenced in any appreciable degree the content of his religious thought.

We have seen that it was chiefly Paul's religious experience that supplied the materials for his theology. His theology springs from his efforts to understand his own life. Always with Paul, religion comes first, and theology second. Experience precedes reflection on experience. To this we must add the witness and teaching of his immediate predecessors in the Faith. He himself acknowledges the help and information he had received from the leaders of the primitive Church.[2]

[1] Cf. Manson, op. cit., p. 186.
[2] I Cor. 11.23–6; 15.3–8. For the continuity of the teaching of the early Church and that of Jesus; see R. H. Fuller, *The Mission and Achievement of Jesus*, pp. 112 f.

It is a mistake to suppose that there is any complete discontinuity between the teaching of Paul and that of the first Apostles. Whatever developments were made by the creative power of Paul's mind, they were present at least in germ in the consciousness of the primitive Christian community.

We see this continuity between Paul's teaching and that of the primitive community in their common teaching about the Lordship of Christ. Bousset in his book *Kyrios Christos* argued that there was a radical difference between the Christology of Palestine and that of the Greek-speaking Church, and that Paul was dependent upon the latter for his own doctrine of Christ.[1] It is not necessary, however, to go out of Palestine to find a community in the very early days of Christianity which worshipped Jesus and addressed him as "Lord". Not only is this title given to Christ but with it are transferred many of the words and phrases which in the Old Testament were used of Yahweh.[2] The Lord Jesus is looked upon as one who is worthy of worship and adoration. The very fact that prayers were addressed to him shows that in their thinking they set Jesus on the side of God,[3] and that they expected him to do what God could do. 1 Cor. 11.20,23, shows that the title κυριός had an established place in the pre-Pauline text of the Eucharist and in the pre-Pauline Creed. The phrase *maran atha'* in 1 Cor. 16.22 shows that it had already found its way into the early liturgy of the Church.[4] Clearly the gulf which is alleged to have existed between Paul and the primitive Church on this matter of the Lordship of Christ is virtually non-existent.

[1] R. Bultmann, in *Primitive Christianity in its Contemporary Setting* (1956), p. 177, also traces Paul's Christological ideas to the mythical cults of Hellenism.

[2] Acts 2.21; 11.16.

[3] Acts 7.59, 60. Cf. κύριε ὁ θεός in Ps. 30.6.

[4] Cf. W. Foerster in *Lord* (Bible Key Words), p. 109: "There is no ground for maintaining that the word [*maran atha*] did not originate with the Palestinian Church, since all the Aramaic words preserved in the gospels did so."

The relationship of Paul to the primitive Church is perhaps most clearly seen in his emphasis upon the death and resurrection of Christ. The belief in the resurrection of Christ was part of the tradition which Paul had received and there are few who would deny continuity of his thought with that of the early Church on this matter. The same unanimity of opinion, however, is not forthcoming in respect to the primitive and Pauline views of the death of Christ. There are those who maintain that the death of Christ in the primitive Church was not in any way related to the divine forgiveness or the salvation of men, and that the Pauline doctrine of Christ's death was his own innovation. It would, however, be arbitrary to suppose that the very early Christians saw significance only in the Resurrection. How could they when the Cross of necessity preceded the Resurrection? The novel element that they had to fit into their new concept of the Messiah—indeed that which made the concept new—was that of suffering and death. It would have been strange, therefore, if they had not sought some rationale of that suffering and death.[1]

While therefore Paul greatly enriched our understanding of Christ and while he spoke of Christ in ways to which there is no precise parallel in our records of the primitive Church, he must have received the germs of his later thought in the teaching of the early Church.

THE CHALLENGE OF A LEGAL RELIGION

If these were the sources of his information upon which he brought to bear his insight and own experience, what was the impulse which led to such creative thinking? It is practically

---

[1] See H. A. A. Kennedy, *The Theology of the Epistles* (1923), pp. 114 ff; E. Stauffer, *New Testament Theology* (E.T. 1955), pp. 129 ff. Cf. the following quotation from Schoeps, op. cit., p.61: "The doctrine of the character of Jesus' death as a sacrificial atonement no doubt goes back to a traditional church formulae, for the idea of the ransom of sinners as a word of the Lord was known to the church."

certain that no one attempts to write as Paul did without some challenge or compulsion from without. In other words, Paul's motive in writing such an epistle as the one to the Romans must have been apologetic. The new spiritual life is summoned to explain and vindicate itself to that which already holds the ground. Similarly, the task of theology to-day and the particular form which it takes springs from the urge to vindicate the Christian conception of the world against the sheer negations of a naturalistic one, whether expressed in materialistic terms or idealistic.

All the theologies of the New Testament are apologetic, and the variety of them, so far from proving that there is any incoherence in early Christianity, only proves the vitality and urgency of the early Christian theologians in meeting every challenge to the Faith. We have a striking instance of this in the work of the Fourth Evangelist. It is clear that he was a man who could be a thinker and appreciate knowledge, stand in the stream of current intellectual movements, and at the same time be a faithful member of the Church. By adopting the term Logos, John showed that in the historical Jesus both Jews and Greeks could find the fulfilment and completion of their own gropings towards the truth. All that the Jews had believed about God as proceeding forth by his word to create and govern nature and to reveal himself to men by his prophets, belongs to Jesus and is consummated in him. All that the Greeks had imagined of a divine activity in the world, all their speculations about a divine mediator between the immutable and timeless God and the created world, also find in Jesus their justification, their fulfilment, and their correction.[1]

To this rule that creative work is the response to a challenge, Paul is no exception. He too thinks out the Christian message in answer to a summons. But the challenge comes to him not from the "Word of God" of the Old Testament nor from the

[1] See my *The Religious Thought of St John* (1950), p. 102.

Logos of Greek philosophy; it comes to him from the Law. Christianity was everything to him because it meant Righteousness, and for this very reason it was challenged persistently and vehemently by those who thought they had the way of Righteousness without it. In all essentials, Paul's theology is a definition of Christianity in relation to, and as a rule in contrast with, legal religion. Sometimes the legal religion is of what we call a ritual type (as in Galatians), though we should remember that the Jew felt a *moral* obligation to keep the ritual law. Sometimes (as in Romans) it is of a moral type, and appeals to the Ten Commandments. In either case, it is by relation to legalism that Paul has to define Christianity; his theology is his response to this challenge. It is a response to a universal challenge, for, in interpreting him we must remember what we have said about the action of the mind upon the categories it employs. Even if there is sometimes a sense in which, in his theologizing, Paul becomes a Jew to the Jews that he may win the Jews, he is not a Jew in religion. He is a man in the first place, and a Christian in the long run, and his vocation as the Apostle of the Gentiles depended on his unique capacity for eliminating the accidental and fixing the permanent and universal—that is the human—elements in Jewish thought and experience. Paul knew from his own experience that a deeper understanding of the Law could lead to a paralysing sense of impotence against the powers of evil.[1] But this is not an exclusively Jewish experience; it is one with which human nature in all ages is familiar. Hence Paul's theology is not only the vindication of Christianity against Judaism, though it was from Judaism that the challenge came; it is a proclamation of the Christian faith as the divine response to the spiritual need and despair of the whole race. For this reason throughout the centuries the fate of the Church has time and again depended on the understanding and evaluation of this letter to the Romans.

[1] See page 43 below.

THE RELEVANCE OF PAUL'S TEACHING FOR TO-DAY

The temptation to become content with a "legalized" and formal religion is one which constantly threatens the Church. Arnold Toynbee emphasizes "the intractability of institutions"[1] and shows how the force of inertia which is inherent in all institutions tends to work against renewal. This temptation arises in a special way in ecclesiastical institutions which are hallowed by antiquity. An opulent society such as ours encourages the spirit of ease and security thus making it increasingly difficult to break through established customs to the hearts of men. In such circumstances as these the way of renewal will not be found in Canon Law or the return to primitive forms of services. The spiritual energy and intelligence which have been devoted to these matters in recent years must be turned to the working out of a theology of redemption such as was proclaimed by Paul in this epistle. His theology is not an antiquarian puzzle, or the solution of problems which can have no interest for us to-day. The circumstances of our day are crying out for an understanding of all that is meant by the word "redemption".

The word "law" may, of course be used in different senses. It may be used of a commandment which regulates men's relations with one another in a society. It is mainly in this sense that we shall be considering law and its attendant dangers in this book. But the word may also be used of scientific affirmations of an observed regularity in nature. Both kinds of laws may be regarded as the expression of ultimate reality and it is when the personal link between them and God is broken that the soul of man is enslaved. The religious man will accept scientific laws as revealing something of the nature of God's universe and he believes that they find their ultimate explanation in the personal will of God. In this case scientific laws will never assume the character of logical necessity or exercise

[1] *A Study of History*, iv, pp. 133 ff.

a tyrannical sway over his life. But there are many people for whom scientific laws are the expression of an ultimate reality that is impersonal and mechanical. This is as soul-destroying as legalism in religion. It is well known, for example, that men have become progressively dependent on the machines which they have built to serve them. The satisfactions afforded by these machines are not necessarily evil (even the Jewish Law was holy), but they are wholly incapable of giving meaning and purpose to life. Men have largely lost the inspiration and loyalties which characterized a simpler and more personal age. They find themselves in the grip of scientific laws which appear to reduce life to a mechanical and determined affair. Professor Harrison Brown of the California Institute of Technology in his book *The Challenge of Man's Future* graphically describes the enslavement of men to their machines. Even the Welfare State, which has provided so many benefits for the individual, tends to make men at all levels to think of themselves as anonymous members of vast statistical groups. The very success of democracy is reducing men to a colourless uniformity. There are those who are aware of their captivity, of their enslavement to these impersonal laws, and struggle to escape. The freedom which they seek often finds expression in licence which is more soul-destroying than the drabness and boredom from which they seek to escape. The reason is that they seek freedom by their own powers. They endeavour to extricate themselves by works; they endeavour to produce their own form of righteousness. In such a situation the message of this epistle is of vital importance.

If it is true that there are some who realize the depth of their frustration and are either consciously or unconsciously asking, What must I do to be saved? it is from this point of view that we must begin our exposition. Paul's central idea, the sum and substance of his gospel, the righteousness of God, cannot be understood by itself; it can only be understood in relation to all the ideas which make one intellectual whole with it. The

order of thought in the epistle invites us first to consider its
negative presuppositions, the necessity for it in the universal
prevalence of sin. Sin, again, is only one in a complex of
Pauline ideas. And if we would have the whole thought of it
present in our minds, as it was to the mind of the Apostle, we
must define it in relation to Law as the embodiment of God's
Will, Wrath, Death, Flesh, and Adam. Only when we have
some adequate conception of the problem presented by sin
defined in this way do we see the conditions which the righteousness of God has to satisfy. From this the Apostle proceeds
to the actual revelation of the righteousness of God, the setting
forth of it, the putting of it within man's reach, in the death of
Christ. The death of Christ itself must in its turn be defined in
all those relations in which sin is defined. It would not, as the
revelation of God's righteousness, meet the problem of sin as
Paul stated it, unless, like sin, it could be defined in relation
to law as the revelation of God's will, to death, and to the
flesh, as well as to the love of God. From the revelation of God's
righteousness we pass on to its appropriation and realization;
in other words, to Paul's doctrine of faith and the new
Christian life. With the doctrine of the new life including, of
course, the assurance of the Spirit and the hope of future
glory, the theology of the epistle in the ordinary sense ter-
minates. But the Apostle does not put down his pen until he
has vindicated the ways of God to men in the face of the
disconcerting historical fact that the mass of God's people
refused to submit to the revelation of his righteousness; and
for him at least, in the circumstances of his time, nothing was
more essential than the daring argument of chapters 9—11.
We shall therefore conclude with a discussion on God's
righteousness in history.

2

THE MORAL LAW

THE central theological conception of this epistle is that of the righteousness of God. The righteousness of God, however, as the sum and substance of his message, is essentially related to sin, and for this reason we must begin our study by considering Paul's teaching about this.

THE TEACHING ABOUT SIN

The Apostle speaks continually of "sin" in the singular, and in all sorts of relations. Out of forty-eight cases in which the word "sin" is used in the epistle, only three are in the plural; and of these two[1] are quotations from the Old Testament. In the Synoptic Gospels, on the other hand, the word is never used in the singular, except in Matt. 12.31, which does not form a real exception, for it is not sin but sins of which Jesus speaks. This suggests that Paul is thinking of sin in a general way; what our Lord speaks of in the concrete, as it comes before him in its particular workings in the lives of individual men, Paul is trying to grasp in its essential nature and wholeness.

This does not mean that there is any loss in vividness or reality. A generalization is only unreal to a man who approaches it from the outside; it is not unreal, empty, or unimpressive, to the man who has had experience of it in his

[1] Rom. 4.7; 11.27.

own being. For this reason Paul does not give us an abstract doctrine of sin, without any bite or challenge: everything he says about it is written out of his heart; it is profoundly, even passionately experimental. It is well that we should insist upon this, for it is sometimes overlooked and people are put off by his appearance of detachment.

The process of generalizing such a concept as sin is indeed a difficult one, the mind finds it much more easy to deal with concrete forms of wrong-doing and sometimes adopts wrong methods when striving to reach the idea of sin as a universal truth. One of these wrong methods is personification. Wishing, for example, to say something which is true not of this or that sin, but sin in general, the mind projects sin, as it were, to a distance at which it can focus it, and then makes assertions as if sin actually had such an independent existence of its own. It generalizes by the simple process of writing Sin with a capital S, and thus bestowing upon it a quasi-personality. Paul himself does this.[1] He does it, possibly, when he says that Sin entered into the world; he does it certainly when he says that Sin reigned in death, and that there is such a thing as a Law of Sin—a law which Sin enjoins as opposed to the law enjoined by God. There are some who say explicitly that Paul teaches that sin is an objective power which may have existed before the Fall.[2] But in our opinion Paul neither affirms nor denies the existence of an evil impulse before the Fall. It seems to us a mistake to distinguish between an "objective" as opposed to a "subjective" doctrine of sin in these passages. We ought to recognize that in this matter there can be nothing "objective" which is not also "subjective". Certainly there is nothing about sin in Paul which cannot be verified in experience; and the places in which there is the appearance of an "objective" view of sin, as a power *in rerum natura* but not in this or that human will, are only those in which Paul on

[1] Rom. 5.12–21; 6.16; 7.17.
[2] See e.g. W. Morgan, *The Religion and Theology of Paul* (1917), p. 18.

the basis of experience generalizes by a kind of poetic personification. "It is not the dark, fatal power, as such that the apostle calls sin, but one's own self-responsible decision against God's command."[1]

Yet everything is not made clear when we say that Paul's doctrine of sin was experimental. The introduction of something else is required, for the question is at once raised. What was the experience in which he gained the insight generalized in this epistle? Was it his experience as a Pharisee when searching for a righteousness of his own? Or was it from his experience as a Christian when he was already in possession of the "righteousness of God"? Or can we perhaps distribute his experience between the two stages of his life, and maintain that he learned somethings about sin by being a sinner, and others only by being saved. All these different answers have been given by theologians at one time or another.

In our opinion the answer depends on what we mean by experience. It is not a *quantum*, something static, but a process, and what it amounts to at any particular moment, supposing it could be arrested, changes in meaning, value, and aspect, as life moves on. It is not at the moment of doing anything that we are aware of the full significance of what we have done; that may come long afterwards and only in the light of different and subsequent experiences. This has to be taken into account when thinking about Paul. When he wrote the Epistle to the Romans he was a Christian and he could not be anything else; we cannot imagine him even for one moment divesting himself of this character. When he writes of sin, he writes, of course, on the basis of experience; no man could do otherwise. But he is not writing a detailed confession of sins committed in the past, as when Augustine tells us that he stole apples, or when Bunyan confesses that he once blasphemed. He is telling us the *universal truth* about sin, as through his own experience he had come to know it. There are those who think

[1] E. Brunner, *The Letter to the Romans* (E.T. 1959), p. 45.

that Paul in Romans 7 was not writing autobiographically,
but symbolically as a description of the life of all Jews. It
seems to us more likely that Paul realizes that his personal
experience is common to all men. But the experience, as he
sees it now, is that of the Christian. Later on we shall consider
whether Rom. 7.14–25 refers to Paul's pre-Christian experiences or to a permanent element in the Christian life;
here we only wish to emphasize that it is the reborn man who
is writing and showing us what sin is in the light of God
universally and essentially. His understanding of sin is
Christian, not pre-Christian or Pharisaic; the true meaning
of sin was not discovered at the feet of Gamaliel, but at the
foot of the Cross. It is in the light of that Christian experience
that Paul speaks about sin with such profundity and heart
searching words.[1] This means that Paul's writings are in-
tensely personal, they cannot lead us back to the pre-Christian
consciousness of sin; we know only what he thought of sin in
the light of his present Christian experience. It would be quite
impossible for a man who had undergone such a conversion
as Paul to look objectively upon the past; the present would
colour all.

Paul nowhere gives us a formal definition of sin: it was too
well known in all its aspects to need that. But it is apparent
from such passages as Rom. 3.20: "through the law cometh
knowledge of sin", and 5.13: "sin is not imputed when there
is no law", that it is defined by relation to law which embodies
the will of God. Sin is the refusal to recognize God as creator
(Rom. 3.23) whose will has been proclaimed in the law. No
doubt if we go back to Paul's experience as a Pharisee, and the
failures of those days (which are surely not excluded by the
boasting of Phil. 3.6: "touching the righteousness which is in
the law found blameless"), the law referred to here is the Law

---

[1] Cf. C. K. Barrett's comment on Rom. 7.25: "The insights of this
paragraph are Christian insights." *A Commentary on the Epistle to the Romans*
(1957), p. 152.

of Moses. It was in the form of the Law of Moses that law
first proved a reality for the Apostle. Not, we may suppose,
because it was *Moses'* law, but because that happened to be
the law which incorporated a standard which belonged to
religion as such. In this case the Law of Moses bore witness
to the common law of man and of the world as well as of God.
"What Paul says of the religion of Judaism, the highest of all
religions, is true *a fortiori* of all religion."[1]

THE GENERALIZATION OF THE LAW

Paul has been charged with inconsistency in his references
to the law.[2] He calls it "holy and righteous and good".[3] He
never fails to regard the Jewish people as favoured because
they had been "instructed out of the law".[4] Over against this
favourable treatment of the law, he speaks of it as that which
held men captive, something from which they were greatly
in need of deliverance.[5] It came, he declares, "that the tres-
pass might abound".[6] The only reasonable explanation to us
for these different attitudes is that more than one meaning is
placed on the word "law". It would seem that Paul looks
upon the Torah, or what he calls ὁ νόμος, under two aspects:
(1) as a system of Mosaic legislation, with all its accumulated
traditions which time had gathered round it, and (2) as the
sum total of all the ethical requirements which God demands
of men in the development of character and the exercise of
true conduct.[7] Paul, of course, did not explicitly distinguish
between the two in the language he used, yet he must have

[1] Barrett, op. cit., p. 140.
[2] E.g. J. W. Parkes, *Jesus, Paul and the Jews* (1936), p. 120.
[3] Rom. 7.12.
[4] Rom. 2.18; 3.1–3.
[5] Rom. 8.6.
[6] Rom. 5.20.
[7] Cf. C. H. Dodd, *The Bible and the Greeks* (1935), p. 35. See also H. W.
Robinson in *Law and Religion* (Ed. E. I. J. Rosenthal, 1938), pp. 50 ff, for
the meaning of Torah which includes both aspects.

done so in his own mind. And it was the latter which he described as "spiritual", and as "holy and righteous and good" and which he perceived to be true for all men, Jews and Gentiles alike. Schoeps[1] maintains that the Law is an integral part of the Covenant and that when Paul isolates the Law from the Covenant he reveals his misunderstanding of the Covenant. But long before Paul, the prophets had foreseen the danger of legalism implied in the Covenant and accordingly looked for a new covenant written on the heart (Hos 2. 19, 20; Jer. 31.32–4; Ezek. 16.60–3; Isaiah 61.8). Paul went behind the formal expression of the Law to a more fundamental understanding of God's will. This is what our Lord did when dealing with the question of divorce (Mark 10.2–12), and in the Sermon on the Mount (Matt. 5.25 ff). It was because he was able to separate the essential and the universal from the temporary and local in Jewish Law that he was able to preach his message of salvation to all men. He brought the charge against everyone that they were under sin.[2] But if sin can only be defined in relation to law, and is, in point of fact defined for Jews by relation to the Mosaic Law, then, in order to put both Jews and Gentiles on the same footing as sinners to whom a righteousness of God is essential, Paul must have seen the necessity of stripping from the Mosaic Law all that was accidental to it; he must be able to generalize the conception of law, and to show that all that was vital in it, everything in virtue of which sin has to be defined in relation to it, has validity for the Gentiles as well as the Jews. We see in the Epistle to the Romans that this is done definitely, though it might seem accidentally, in various ways.

It is done, for example, in the passage: "that which may be known of God is manifest in them; for God manifested it to them. For the invisible things of him since the creation of the world are clearly seen, being perceived through the things

[1] *Paul*, pp. 213 ff.
[2] Rom. 3.9.

that are made, even his everlasting power and divinity."[1]
Here the Apostle argues that, in the constitution of nature and
in man's relation to it, there is such a revelation of God given
as puts man under a religious and therefore under a moral
obligation to God, and renders him inexcusable—we may even
say, from the theological standpoint of the Apostle, was meant
to render him inexcusable—if he failed to satisfy these obligations. In this he was in accordance not only with Jewish thought,
but with contemporary Greek philosophy. The argument from
design had become habitual in the Schools, having been
stated first of all with transparent simplicity by Xenophon
in his account of the reasoning of Socrates.[2] Paul finds in
this instinctive reference from nature up to nature's God, "a
testimony of the soul naturally Christian". He is able, at
Lystra and Athens, to assume that men will respond to it.

It is true that the word "law" is not used in this passage.
But when we are confronted with a revelation of God's eternal
power which stimulates in man a mood of adoring wonder,
and when we see that the failure to respond to that revelation
issues in deep moral degradation, how else can we describe
the conditions under which men live other than by saying
that they live under a law. True, it is not the Mosaic Law; it is
not an institution or a code. But it is a divine law which is
recognized by men whose minds and consciences are alert.
Its recognition carries with it a duty of obligation towards
God as effectively as the Mosaic Law did for the Jews. According to Paul, there were some in the Greek world who thought
that the failure to respond to such a revelation of the law of
God made them worthy of extreme punishment.[3] Man

---

[1] Rom. 1.19 f.

[2] Xenephon, *Mem.* 1.4.3 ff; see also, *Corp. Herm.* 5.6 ff; Ps.-Arist. *De
Mundo* 6.25; and in Judaism, *Wisdom* 7.5, Philo. *De Decal* 59 f.

[3] Rom. 1.32. Cf. the following passage from Pseudo-Heraclitus (a contemporary of Paul), *Letter* 9.91: "If a man transgresses what the law imposes, he will be impious; or rather he will not dare transgress; for he
could not escape. Justice has many furies, watch dogs for sin."

knows indeed the divine command, just as he knows God from the revelation of his works, yet often he takes no notice of the command but lives almost defiantly in opposition to God's will. But the fact that there is this universal law enables Paul to preach his Gospel with hope that some will hear and respond.

This is completely different from the standpoint adopted by Rudolf Bultmann. He argues that neither nature nor history is capable of supplying the positive, revelatory complement of the soul's innate knowledge of God, not merely because of the perverse attitude of the fallen creature towards his world, but because nature and history are inherently barren. Bultmann sees nature primarily as a network of causal relationships, necessary to man's domestic life, but a snare to his spirit. History, he says, as an economy in the patristic sense is a fiction, for it is intrinsically ambiguous. Together nature-history forms a single profane territory of objective knowledge and experience, a quarter from which divine revelation cannot come.[1] It is clear that Paul would have had some fairly strong things to say if Bultmann had been his contemporary!

We find a more explicit generalizing of the law in Rom. 2.14: "When Gentiles which have no law do by nature the things of the law, these, having no law, are a law unto themselves; in that they show the work of the law written in their hearts, their conscience bearing witness therewith, and their thoughts one with another accusing or else excusing them." Karl Barth argues that this passage can refer only to Gentile Christians, who are a law to themselves because they have received the Spirit of Christ. "They are Gentile *Christians* to whom, through God's wonderful deed in Jesus Christ, the very thing has happened which those prophetic words promised to the people of Israel. To them God has given his Holy Spirit in such a manner that they can now do it and

[1] See "Christianity and History", by the present writer, in *Church Quarterly Review*, October 1960.

carry it out."[1] But both φύσει in verse 14 and κατηγορούντων in verse 15 are inconsistent with such an idea. The Jew rested on his law and the point of this passage is that what the law ought to have produced among the Jews and did not, was produced sometimes among the Gentiles, where the law of the Jews had never been heard of.

Paul is here referring to what theologians call the "law of Nature". This term, of course, has a very different connotation from that which obtains in popular thought to-day. Nature is assumed to mean the objective material world, and laws of nature are understood to refer to the sequences of cause and effect which are observable in the world of matter. It was otherwise in Paul's day. Man was then considered to be included in the realm of nature in the sense that his happiness and well-being depended on his being governed by a certain natural law which was eternal and issued from God; just as to many scientists the body of laws under which the material universe is subsumed is the expression of a reality above and beyond the mass of phenomena, which by these laws are reduced to order and comprehended.

It is in Stoic theology that we find the clearest expression of this law of nature. In Paul's day the Aristotelian conception of two kinds of men, the essentially free and the essentially unfree had given way to a conception of mankind as a real universe. Men might still differ from one another in various ways, but they believed that they shared a common humanity. The Stoics were the first preachers in the pagan world of this cosmopolitanism. It was the business, they said, of human beings to recognize the universe as governed by universal law. The Creator, immanent in all his works, must regard the

---

[1] *A Shorter Commentary on Romans* (E.T. 1959), p. 36 f. Gustaf Wingren in his *Theology in Conflict* charges Barth with having forgotten Paul's teaching about the law which is written in all men's heart's, so that they are without excuse before God. The Noachian covenant may have been Paul's warrant for this reference to Gentile capacity to do by nature the things of the Law. This Covenant was made with all mankind through Noah.

interests of all equally and men are to be, as it were, in league with him, to merge self in the universal order, to think only of that and its welfare. The virtuous life is the life according to nature, i.e. according to one universal law; such a life alone is the worthy aim of all those who look upon the world as their city.

There is in Cicero's *Republic*[1] a good expression of this Natural Law working in the hearts of those who owed no obligation to the Mosaic Law:

> There is a true law which is right reason, agreeable to nature, diffused among all men, constant, eternal, which calls us to duty by its injunctions, and by its prohibitions deters us from wrong; which upon the good lays neither injunction nor prohibition in vain; while for the bad neither its injunctions nor its prohibitions avail at all. This law admits neither of addition nor subtraction nor abrogation. The vote of neither Senate nor people can discharge us from our obligation to it. We are not to look for some other person to expound or interpret it; nor will there be one law for Rome and another for Athens, nor one at this date and another later on; but one law shall embrace all races over all time, eternal and immortal; and there shall be hereby one common master and commander of all—God who originated this law and proposed it and arbitrates concerning it; and if any one obeys it not, he shall play false to himself and shall do despite to the nature of man, and by this very fact shall pay the greatest penalties, even if he should escape all else that is reckoned punishment.

That is the kind of thing Paul must have had in mind when he wrote about the law in his Epistle to the Romans. There are Gentiles who do "by nature" the things of the Jewish Law. They have the "work which the law prescribes written on their hearts". They were aware also of a conscience which passes judgement on their actions—an internal remorse, fear, or shame which follows upon the breaking of the moral law.[2]

---

[1] *Republic* 3.22; Cf. Lactantius, *Div. Inst.* 6.8.
[2] See pp. 52 f below.

They were capable of strict self-examination, bringing accusations against their personal behaviour. Paul is unable to interpret the presence of a moral law at work among the Gentiles as among the Jews without subsuming it under the category of law; but in the very act of doing so, the law loses its limited, Jewish, historical character and becomes a matter of universal significance.

It may also be said that the passage at the end of chapter 2, in which Paul distinguishes between the Jew outwardly and the Jew inwardly, rests upon this enlarging and spiritual-izing of the conception of law. The Jew inwardly is in fact the man to whom that which is simply Jewish in the law has no longer any importance; it is not its historical but its eternal content, not its national but its divine and human significance, which really matters. The justice which springs from the moral law may be observed by the Gentile: and accordingly, so far from the law in this sense being that which separates the Gentile from the Jew, it is the common ground on which both Jew and Gentile can meet on equal terms. All men, according to Paul, are under the law and are under an obligation to keep that law. But in fact, all men, Jews and Gentiles, have failed to keep their obligations and are therefore all under sin. It is from the last proposition that Paul starts and it is in the work-ing out of its logical implications that he attains to the conception of a universal moral law.

It is of great importance that we should grasp this part of Paul's thinking, for it is that which underlies all that follows. It is that which makes his epistle possess universal relevance. The moral world would be unintelligible and incoherent to him without this conception of a universal moral law. Indeed there could be no moral world without it. To banish this generalized conception of the law which determines the rela-tions between God and man would make both religion and morality impossible. Because this truth is so often overlooked, Paul has been misrepresented and misunderstood. It is said, for example, that Paul inherited from Pharisaism certain legal conceptions of the relations between man and God, and that, though he rose above this conception in his spiritual experience, he was never able dialectically to transcend it in his thoughts.[1] His theology, it is said, always begins from a forensic and judicial basis. It is this legalistic attitude which puts people "off", it is so different, they say, from the attitude of Jesus. It is this misunderstanding of Paul which gives rise to the idea that he began his thinking about the atonement from a Pharisaic idea of the relations between man and God instead of with Christian presuppositions.

It seems to us that this whole line of thought arises from a complete misunderstanding of Paul's teaching. We have seen in this chapter that Paul did not base his theology upon the historical Jewish conception of the law. It is true that the Rabbis represented the relations between God and man in a legal manner. In the time of Paul legal righteousness had become a substitute for a personal relationship with God. So meticulous had the leaders of religion become in their observances that numerous definitions and amplifications had been added until the Pentateuch had been overlaid with a mass of rabbinic tradition all of which was equally binding. The law had become a yoke and a burden.

But Paul, as we have seen, clearly transcended this conception of the law. In his mind he generalized the law as something determining the relations of God and man universally, something without which the moral life of man would have been impossible. But in this generalized sense law is not open to the abuse which is often levelled at it on the ground that it destroys true religion. It is not "forensic", it is not "judicial", it is not even "legal". These question-begging epithets are quite beside the mark. The law, according to Paul, is universal, it is human, it is divine, it is moral. As the form in which the

[1] See e.g. Joseph Klausner's *From Jesus to Paul* (1945), a book which interprets Paul without much reference to Paul's religious experience.

will of God presents itself to the conscience of mankind, it has an inevitable, searching, personal power of self-application to persons and situations which transcend the forensic or legal approach. As the moral obligation to which man's consciousness bears witness even among the Gentiles, as we have seen, it is free from that element of the arbitrary and temporary which marks human laws and decrees. As Cicero said there is not "one law for Rome and another for Athens, nor one at this date and another later on; but one law embraces all races over all time, eternal and immortal".

THE OBLIGATION OF THE LAW

This single law may be described as the "categorical imperative" of Kant. All men pursue some end which at least they represent to themselves as "good". The content of this "good" may and does vary from place to place and from time to time. Hedonists maintain that the good means some condition of self-satisfaction. Utilitarians hold that the good is not the individual's own satisfaction, but "the greatest happiness of the greatest number". Actions, in this case, are good in so far as they tend to promote the most desirable condition of the greatest possible number of human beings. Intuitionists fall back on the irreducible and ultimate verdict of the moral sense; the good is that which is directly "given" in the moral consciousness. Others identify the good with self-realization, with the satisfaction of all man's desires. This is what Walter Lippmann calls the equilibrium of balanced excesses.[1]

We may say, speaking generally, that the good always involves the subordination of the interests of the isolated self to those of some wider whole. Even when this social reference is not obvious, it is always present. There is very deep meaning

[1] *Preface to Morals*, p. 279.

over the penitent sinner. It is in the light of this one divine
law that God judges men according to their works, that is,
according to the manner in which in their life they have
responded to, and satisfied, that law in virtue of which their
relations to God possess any moral value at all.[1]

[1] It is interesting to notice that John also summarized Christian behaviour in terms of the law, the *commandment* of love. By including all
commandments under the one commandment of love, John dissolved the
whole conception of Jewish legalism. This does not mean that the idea of
law or obligation is ruled out. See my *The Religious Thought of St John*,
pp. 244 ff.

3

THE UNIVERSALITY OF SIN

THE UNIVERSALITY OF SIN

So far we have been concerned with the way in which Paul universalized the conception of law. This also implies the universality of sin for Paul brings the idea of sin into close relation with that of law. But we do not really appreciate what he meant by sin unless we trace the interaction of law and sin in his experience. As soon as we attempt to do this a difficulty recurs by which we are often haunted in the study of his letters. Paul had his experience of the law under a definite form—that of the Law of Moses; that was for him the most obvious and probably the only embodiment open to him. But the Law of Moses cannot be reproduced by us. We cannot put ourselves into the position of a man brought up in a Pharisaic environment, and confronted with the statutes of the Penta-teuch and the traditions of the elders. We cannot imagine ourselves being expected to even try to achieve by the perfect observance of all these traditions a righteousness of our own which might win the approval of God. Life under the law is completely foreign to us. The question, therefore, arises: if Paul's teaching arose out of an experience so alien to us, how can it carry any authority for us?

The answer to this difficulty has already been suggested in the previous chapter. That there is an adequate answer is involved in the fact that, in spite of the distinctive experiences of Paul within Judaism, he was able to eliminate their peculiarities, to universalize them and on the strength of this broadening of the basis of his religious experience, he was able to address himself with confidence to the common conscience of mankind. That universal law which, in the previous chapter, was seen to determine for him all the relations of God and man, and by so doing to make them relations of moral value, takes shape variously according to man's circumstances and history. For Paul, the law took shape, defined itself with divine authority, in the Law of Moses; for other men of other ages it takes other forms. But all its manifestations, whatever the adequacy or inadequacy, assume a sense of the *sacred* which demands obedience.[1] Every law, in other words, appealed to men because somehow or other, the voice of God was heard speaking through it. It is this which gives sin the same character, no matter what its particular content may be. No things could be more unlike the vices of paganism which are pilloried in the first chapter of Romans, and the high moral pretensions of the self-righteous Jews which are attacked in the second chapter. But there is one relation in which they are identical—their relation to the eternal law of God. Hence the term "sin" belongs to the vocabulary of religion, not to that of moral or political philosophy. To the atheist sin can only appear to be an illusion. "Against Thee only have I sinned" is always the cry of the awakened sinner. The one constant element in the meaning of sin is that it puts a man out of fellowship with God.

If Paul had not been able to generalize both law and sin in such a way as to include both Jews and Gentiles, he would have had no catholic gospel to preach; his writings would have remained a curious relic of spiritual autobiography. But the very fact that he could so generalize them proves that his experience of the Mosaic Law is in its very nature and essence akin to something which is characteristic of human nature as a

[1] What Otto calls "numinous awe", *The Idea of the Holy*, p. 130.

whole. It is, furthermore, a fact that the finest examples of human sainthood have emerged from the recognition of this very truth. The highest and most spiritual life which is available to man is one which starts with the assertion of universal sinfulness. Sainthood seems to be inseparable from the confession of sin, and the power which works with such efficacy in holy people is the experience of the forgiveness of sins. Accordingly what Paul writes about sin we do not expect to be unintelligible or unreal, on the contrary, as the experiences of Luther, Wesley, and others have shown, what he says can find a response in our own hearts.

Paul was aware of what so many modern thinkers have ignored, namely, that before being saved man must realize that he is a sinner. The existential anguish of man must be so deep that he realizes that salvation by science, politics, or sociology is too superficial for his needs. Only when he knows that he is lost will he appreciate the wonder of God's grace. It is against this background of thought that we will understand Paul's teaching about sin and its consequences.

THE INTERACTION OF SIN AND LAW

What, then, does Paul say about the relation and interaction of sin and law in his (and perhaps in our own) experience?

He has much to say which implies that there is a close connection between them, much which may seem unflattering to the law, and he takes care to make it plain that for the law in itself he has nothing but the most religious respect. The law is ἅγιος, holy; that is, it is God's law. The commandment in which it is expressed on any given occasion is holy and just and good. The natural and proper end of the commandment, that which God has in view in bringing it into man's consciousness, is life.[1] If the law given by God had been able to give life, there would have been no need for the gospel.[2]

[1] Rom. 7.10.
[2] Gal. 3.21.

Paul does not say that it is the fault of the law that this result was not attained. On the contrary, the law's incapacity is not to be referred to itself, but to the subject with which it has to deal.[1] The one thing that has to be kept in mind at every point is that the law of God, defining itself variously in the consciences of men, is always conceived as confronting men with an *imperative*. It is part of its very nature to make a demand —an absolutely righteous demand, yet in the last resort a demand—not an inspiration. The divine law reveals its power in three ways:

(*a*) When a man lives under the law in this sense, the first result of it is that he comes to the consciousness of sin. When Paul pronounces sentence "through the law cometh the knowledge of sin",[2] he speaks no doubt as a Christian. His Christian intelligence enables him to focus the meaning of his pre-Christian experiences as he might not have been able to do in his pre-Christian days. We cannot deny that there is such a thing as blind, Pharisaic self-righteousness produced under the law; but the law does not produce this any more than it does sensuality or other sins. Its true result is an ever deepening consciousness that life is not in right relation to God; it is wrong with God, and no divine righteousness can be realized in it. The Jews had the law of God made real to them through their Scriptures and their history with a vividness to which no other nation presents a parallel. Within the Bible, it is true, we find a development in the idea of sin *pari passu* with a development in the understanding of God. We find a similar development in the life of Paul. So long as he thought of righteousness as external conformity to the law of God he could confidently claim that "as touching the righteousness which is in the law" he was "found blameless". He was complete, consistent, and for a time at least a

[1] Rom. 8.13.
[2] Rom. 3.20.

contented Pharisee. As, however, he advanced in Judaism,[1] he made a great discovery. He noticed for the first time that one of the commandments forbade coveting,[2] that is to say, that a mere feeling, a state of the heart which cannot be seen by outsiders, was condemned as sin. It includes every kind of immoral desire. Whatever may be the meaning of this word (ἐπιθυμία)[3] when it was brought home to Paul that the law was not confined to outward acts, but included inward dispositions, that one of the commandments forbade evil desire as well as action, then the battlefield of his moral life was changed. In the realm of action he had hitherto believed himself victorious, in the dominion of the inner life he found himself defeated. This extension of the scope of the law he could not but approve, even though it brought him self-condemnation instead of self-satisfaction. Whenever the divine law pierces through external acts to the springs of the moral life it convicts us of failure.

There is some doubt as to whether the passage in Rom. 7.7 ff is biographical or not.[4] Leenhardt argues that the "I" in this passage means "we". Paul is speaking, he says, of an experience which is general and collective in the same way as the psalmists were accustomed to speak in the first person to express the corporate mind of Israel.[5] On the other hand C. H. Dodd in his commentary maintains that the passage does describe Paul's own experience. And he points out that Paul rarely, if ever, says "I" unless he is really speaking of himself personally, even if he means to generalize from the particular instance.[6] It is probable that Paul looking into his

---

[1] Gal. 1.14.

[2] Rom. 7.7.

[3] Cf. Matt. 5.28.

[4] See E. Stauffer, *Theologisches Wörterbuch zum Neuen Testament*, ii, pp. 335 ff.

[5] F. J. Leenhardt, *The Epistle to the Romans*, pp. 180 ff. Cf. Schoeps, *Paul*, pp. 183 ff.

[6] *The Epistle to the Romans* (1932), p. 107.

own soul realized that what he had personally experienced was something characteristic of all men who submit themselves to the law of God. It makes a man aware of sin, even if it does not bring it into existence.

Anders Nygren in his commentary[1] denies that Rom. 7.14-25 is an expression of Paul's pre-Christian experiences, and that he is writing of a permanent element in the Christian life. He points out that in 7.1-13 Paul uses the past tense and that in verses 14-25 he changes to the present tense, showing that he is referring to a present Christian experience and not one in the past. Furthermore, throughout chapters 5—8, Paul is writing about the Christian life and it would be strange, he argues, if Paul should suddenly interpolate a passage on "the anguished and discordant status of the soul of a man who is under the law" in such a context. It is more likely, says Nygren, that Paul is here writing of the Christian life, as is the case of the verses which precede and follow. Gal. 5.17 shows that tensions and failures not unlike those described in Rom. 7.14-25 may be experienced by the Christian. Indeed, as long as the Christian lives in the world "he lives as a sinner among sinners, not as a saint among sinners". There is also the difficulty of 7.25. After a confident affirmation of victory over sin, Paul seems to suggest that he suffers moral defeat even at the present time: "So then I myself with the mind serve the law of God; but with the flesh the law of sin." Dodd finds this verse so difficult to reconcile with the theory that verses 14-25 refer to past Christian experiences, that he proposes to move it (without any manuscript evidence) to follow the end of verse 23.[2]

The alternative translation of verse 25 in the New English Bible suggests that the difficulties suggested by Nygren against verses 14-25 being a record of Paul's pre-Christian experiences are not insuperable. The translation is as follows:

[1] *A Commentary on Romans* (1952), pp. 284 ff.
[2] Op. cit., pp. 114 f.

"Thus, left to myself,[1] while subject to God's law as a rational being, I am yet, in my unspiritual nature, a slave to the law of sin." This shows clearly that Paul is confessing that when he is left to himself, when he has no spiritual support which comes from constant reliance on the grace of God, he falls back into his pre-Christian condition which he has just described. In Rom. 7.14–25 he writes of the man who is "not in Christ". He draws upon his own experiences before he came to rely entirely upon Christ, but he also realizes that what was true of his past may also be true of the present if he lapses from the faith. The use of the present tense throughout verses 14–25 shows that Paul is not writing *merely* of the past, but of a characteristic of human nature which is potentially always present and which becomes an awful reality when a man relies upon his own strength instead of the grace of God in Christ. The fact that Paul in verses 1–24 makes no mention of Christ or the Holy Spirit suggests that he is thinking of a period when he was not aware of the help which comes from either. In chapter 8 when Paul is speaking clearly of the Christian life the name of Christ occurs three times in the first three verses and the Spirit is frequently mentioned in the following verses. From this point of view verse 25 is a warning that without the grace of God reinforcing man's unspiritual nature he quickly falls back into the captivity of sin.

For these reasons, in spite of Nygren's criticisms, we think it is reasonable to suppose that in this chapter we have a vivid account of Paul's pre-Christian experiences, before he was "in Christ" and still under the law. The law convicted him of moral failure which in his own experience could only be overcome through constant reliance upon Christ.[2]

(*b*) Law reveals its power in another way; as Paul puts it, it

---

[1] This brings out the force of αὐτὸς ἐγώ.

[2] A similar account of the perplexity of a man who seeks to observe the law and yet finds it important to overcome sin will be found in 2 Esdras. 9.32–6.

works wrath.[1] In the Epistle to the Romans there are several references to the wrath of God. Two of these must be interpreted as having an eschatological meaning.[2] God's wrath is something which will be clearly revealed in the Last Day. But eschatological ideas do not arise out of nothing; they are at least the projection in imagination of something which the conscience knows to be real. Accordingly Rom. 1.18 implies that God's wrath is being executed in the present, although even here we must not dismiss the possibility that in the present men are already beginning to taste the experience of that eschatological expectation yet to be revealed. It is due to the forbearance of God that he delays the final execution of his wrath.[3]

What does Paul mean by the revelation of God's wrath? That God is hostile to sinful men, expressing anger after the fashion of human passions, must be ruled out, although this has been suggested.[4] It is frequently assumed in popular opinion that according to Paul, God, in the exercise of his wrath, lays aside temporarily his love and acts like one who has lost his temper. Nothing could be further from Paul's teaching. All that we mean when we speak of the consequences of sin, Paul meant when he spoke of the wrath of God. The laws of God which articulate his demands cannot be violated without serious moral or physical consequences. When men choose to ignore God, to prefer darkness to the light of truth and goodness, they condemn themselves and inevitably reap the harvest of their sins in morally debased and disintegrated personalities.[5] People who violate natural laws do not break them. They themselves are broken by the laws in operation. So also is it, according to Paul, with all moral and spiritual laws. Their violation brings moral and physical wreckage

[1] Rom. 4.15.
[2] Rom. 2.5 and 5.9.
[3] Rom. 4.22.
[4] W. Sanday and A. C. Headlam, *Romans*, p. 129.
[5] See my *The Meaning of Salvation*, pp. 25 ff.

which constitutes the divine reaction against all ungodliness.

This "wrath of God" must not be regarded as an automatic mechanical process.[1] The wrath of God is the wrath of a divine personality, but does not exhaust the activity of that personality. The universe is moral and it is God's world; in whatever sphere they operate, its laws are his and are the expression of his will. But what if that will and purpose is to bestow love upon creation in order to accomplish its redemption? Then the "wrath of God" takes on a deeper meaning and becomes the negative aspect of all the good which God purposed for mankind. Wrath is then the obverse of the divine love and grace, and represents not personal anger or vengeance, but because it is the consequence of a broken personal relationship, involves the deepest sorrow of the Father's heart. In this we have the basis of the redeeming action which, according to Paul, God took in Jesus Christ whereby a man can be redeemed from sin and wrath and death.

(c) "The wage of sin is death." There is probably no question on which more that is misleading has been written than the question, What did Paul mean by death? Modern minds tend to make distinctions, such as spiritual, temporal, and eternal death. But Paul did not distinguish between the spiritual and physical aspects of death.[2] Man was man to him, an indivisible whole, and to introduce such distinctions in the interpretations of this epistle would be wrong. It is equally misleading, though widely accepted, to suggest that the connection of sin and death for Paul rests on a literal inter-

[1] Cf. C. K. Barrett, *Romans*, p. 33. In contrast see Dodd, op. cit., p. 23: "The inevitable process of cause and effect in a moral universe", and A. T. Hanson, *The Wrath of the Lamb* (1957), pp. 68 ff.

[2] Cf. H. A. A. Kennedy, *The Theology of the Epistles* (1923), p. 127: "There is little doubt that when Paul speaks of death, he regards it synthetically, not distinguishing as we are wont to do, between its physical and spiritual aspects, but viewing the experience in its entirety, as involving primarily separation from God."

pretation of the opening chapters of Genesis, and that we are only at his point of view when we assume that death was attached to sin in the same way as any penalty is attached by a human legislature to the violation of its laws, and that but for this statutory arrangement man's relation to death might have been quite other than it is. In spite of the references to Gen. 3 in Rom. 5.12 ff, it is doubtful if Paul ever raised the abstract questions here suggested. The story of the Fall and its consequences, including the connection between death and sin, produces no impression at all until it produces an impression on conscience, and that impression is one which attests itself.[1] It is through the experience of sin and law and wrath, that we learn the full meaning of the words, "the wages of sin is death".[2] The mortality of man is a natural characteristic, but the death of a sinner is tragic. It is not to be assimilated to any natural event; its real nature is only to be discovered in the conscience, and to conscience it is never anything else but a doom. It has to be interpreted in relation to sin and law, and in this relation the fact of God's judgement cannot be left out. Thoughts and experiences like these and not references to Genesis 3, give authority to what Paul says of death in connection with sin. What he says can be verified

[1] This should be taken into consideration in discussion on the doctrine of sin in relation to Infant Baptism.

[2] Barrett, op. cit., pp. 111 f, raises the question, "What if there are men who do not sin?" and points out that this is not a hypothetical question for "the only means of estimating sin is transgressable law" and no law existed between Adam and Moses. He suggests that a pointer to the solution of the dilemma may be found in the distinction between sin and transgression, "Sin is turned into transgression (and can then lead to death) . . . only when a law is given." Cf. F. J. Leenhardt, *The Epistle to the Romans*, p. 146, "In the absence of the knowledge of the will of God, sin has not the full dimensions of the sin of Adam. It is a material but not a formal sin." On the other hand, we must remember the implications of the wider meaning given by Paul to the law which we discussed above, pp. 28 ff. The heathen "do by nature the things of the law" (Rom. 2.14,15, cf. 5.14), and this was characteristic of all men before the Mosaic Law was given.

not by an appeal to Genesis, but by an appeal to one's own conscience.

The death of a sinner is sin which has worked out its own end. Sin does entail certain results which can be separated and distinguished from it. These temporal results of sin may even be remedial in nature and it would be contrary to our true good to desire to be relieved of these. But Paul's teaching is something much deeper than this. He means that sin persisted in *is* death, separation from God. And salvation from sin means precisely that deliverance from separation from God into union with him, the passage from death to life.

THE NEGATIVE PRESUPPOSITIONS OF THE GOSPEL

There is nothing distinctively Pauline in this, though we owe it to the spiritual insight of Paul that we have been made thoroughly aware of it. Sin, wrath, and death, in their relations to one another and to the law of God, are not Pauline, nor Jewish, not even "legal", they are human and universal. We know what they mean when Paul writes about them and Paul knew that his own experience was not something peculiar to himself, but something which when uttered with passion and eloquence, would awaken echoes in every conscience. He lays great emphasis on the universality of sin[1] —in other words, on the negative presupposition of the gospel; and in this epistle he proves it in four ways.

First, there is the empirical proof which is worked out in chapters 1 and 2. In chapter 1 Paul adduces evidence of the sinfulness of the Gentiles; in chapter 2 he demonstrates that no appeal to historical privileges can exempt the Jew from the same condemnation. Strictly speaking, no empirical proof

[1] The importance of emphasizing this point will be appreciated from the following quotation from Dietrich Bonhoeffer's *The Cost of Discipleship* (1948), p. 44: "The justification of the sinner degenerated into the justification of sin and the world." An apt description of the twentieth century though Bonhoeffer was speaking about the Reformation.

can establish a universal conclusion, but Paul assumes that no serious person will plead, Not Guilty. He charges all, as he expresses it in chapter 3.9, with being under sin, and he is confident that conscience will give the verdict in his favour.

The section 1.18–32 is too broad and deep for an argument intended only to serve some occasional purpose arising out of the special circumstances of the conditions at Rome. Had it been his main purpose to remove the prejudices and abate the claims of the Jewish Christians, there would have been no adequate reason for this elaborate picture of the pagan world. So terrible an indictment of sins against God and against nature, from some of the worst of which the Jews were comparatively free, must have been intended to touch the pagan world. His motive, which we can now clearly discern, was simply the desire to win from all a favourable hearing for a gospel which must at the outset have been unwelcome both to Jew and Gentile, and more especially to the Jew, because it was prompted by the fact that all alike are under sin, and exposed to God's wrath. The same motive explains why the order of verse 7 is reversed, and the Gentile first pronounced guilty with, no doubt, the full assent of the Jews, who suddenly find themselves involved in the same condemnation.

The conclusion is that all men, Jews and Gentiles alike, are involved in sin, are under the wrath of God, and are in utter need of a deliverance which they are incapable of procuring for themselves.

To this is added a Scriptural proof in chapter 3.10 ff as follows:

There is none righteous, no, not one;
There is none that understandeth,
There is none that seeketh after God;
They have all turned aside, they are together
    become unprofitable;
There is none that doeth good, no, not so much as one:
Their throat is an open sepulchre;
With their tongues they have used deceit:

The poison of asps is under their lips:
Whose mouth is full of cursing and bitterness:
Their feet are swift to shed blood;
Destruction and misery are in their ways;
And the way of peace have they not known:
There is no fear of God before their eyes.

Paul is here following the recognized Hebrew practice of stringing together a number of separate texts—Ps. 14.1–3; 5.9; 140.3; 10.7, Isa. 59.7,8; Ps. 36.1. The passages do not in the first instance refer to all men or to all times, but only to ages in the history of Israel when tyranny or idolatry prevailed. But Paul does not think of what they referred to as originally written. It is his own mind he is expressing by them, the mind of a Christian and an Apostle about the condition of the human race, and the significant thing is that such a judgement can be expressed in words from the Bible. Logically, it may be said, the quotations prove nothing. That is true; but they are addressed not to the logical faculties, but to the conscience; and the Apostle believes that in every man conscience will assent to the impeachment. If everybody who reads the indictment pleads guilty and suffers spiritual agony—as Paul expected them to do—it does not matter whether there is a logical flaw in it or not.

Conscience, according to Paul, is something very different from what we call conscience to-day. The moral theologian would say that conscience is a faculty innate in man which enables him to pass judgement upon his own actions and those of other people. But a careful examination of the passages in which the word "conscience" occurs in the epistles of Paul, such as that carried out by C. A. Pierce in *Conscience in the New Testament* will show that it is a kind of internalized ὀργή. It is the painful consciousness that what one is doing or has done is wrong. Man is by nature so constituted that if he breaks the moral laws of society he will feel an internal pain which punishes him for his wrong doing. The Gentiles were aware of this experience. Euripides, for example, describes συνείδησις as a disease from which Orestes suffers as a result of his crime of slaying his mother Clytemnestra, and which was destroying him.[1]

So the quotation which Paul makes from the Old Testament Scriptures, if it expressed the moral situation at all correctly, was sure to make some impression on his Gentile readers. And even if it is true, as we have already pointed out, that the pagan world was not wholly bad, a Stoic philosopher named Heraclitus, who was a contemporary of Paul, gave a picture of society as lawless and degenerate as that given by the Christian Apostle. They themselves believed that such conduct would lead to pain, or what Paul would call an internal wrath which was indeed the wrath of God.

But Paul has a religious argument for the universality of sin. This is expressed in chapter 3.23 ff: "all have sinned, and fall short of the glory of God, being justified freely by his grace." This is an inference from the one way in which men can be put right with God to the antecedent condition in which they find themselves. If the only way of justification is the one which Paul had experienced and which he preached—justification by the grace of God—then plainly there can be no such thing as justification by the works of the law; in other words, the true and normal relations between God and man, as the law determines them, have nowhere been satisfied. It may be said that this is reasoning in a circle: all men have sinned, and therefore justification must be by grace; and again, justification is by grace, and therefore all men have sinned. But reasoning in a circle is not always wrong. It is not wrong when the circle in which we reason is one which includes within it the whole world of realities with which we are for the time being concerned. There can be nothing outside that circle, no

[1] Quoted by C. A. Pierce in *Conscience in the New Testament* (1955), p. 47, from a number of other passages in classical literature which bring out the same point, namely that συνείδησις is basically a pain.

situation beyond that with which we are concerned. Now this is the case here; and when Paul starting with the primary certainty of his Christian experience, that there is only one way of salvation, argues to the universality of sin, his circle is quite legitimate. If the offer of salvation has been made then there must be need for it. If there is one gospel to be preached to all men—and to Paul nothing was more certain—it is an immediate inference that everyone is in the condition which makes the preaching of the gospel necessary, namely, in a state of sin.

But beside the empirical, scriptural, and religious arguments, Paul has another, which we may call the ethical, and it is associated with his use of the term "flesh". One almost shrinks from discussing a word which has provoked so many different interpretations.[1] But whatever else the word signifies it is something which is common to all men and we feel that however much we refine the ethical meaning in the writings of Paul, the ordinary, even popular, foundation of the term must not be overlooked. In human nature Paul discovers a fundamental weakness and failure and imperfection which is a sign of its having come under the sway of evil. This Paul learned from his own experience,[2] and also from his observation of the world about him, the moral corruption of which he analyses so terribly, and yet so profoundly, in chapters 1 and 2. By some means the flesh has fallen under the domination of sin, making it not merely morally indifferent, but antagonistic to God. He did not, however, believe that sin belonged to the "flesh" as such, though the flesh was the place where weakness and sin manifested themselves most clearly. "Though flesh is not in itself evil sin invades man through it, finding the easiest entry there. Sin may then grow strong in the flesh and cause havoc in every department of life. It may create a lower nature in the flesh to war constantly with the divine inspira-

---

[1] See further pp. 130 ff below.
[2] Rom. 7.

tion and to bring about a state of tension and self-contradiction."[1] This involves something more than just saying that the sum of human instincts has been wrongly directed.[2] "Flesh", for Paul, indicates, at times ordinary human weakness and at other times human nature as it has organized itself apart from God, and this human nature includes the flesh as well as the mind and spirit. The flesh, understood, in this comprehensive way, represents for Paul the virulence and constitutional character as well as the omnipresence of sin; it always carries with it the feeling of despair.

It is in expounding the law and the flesh in their interaction that Paul says the most daring and paradoxical things about sin. The law, he indirectly suggests in Rom. 8.3, might have done something great for man, but it was weak through the flesh; the flesh disabled it. Instead of subduing the flesh, the law irritated it. It acted in a way that seemed to defeat its own end. All that its "thou shalt not" produced from the flesh was "I will". The forbidden fruit is the very fruit we want to eat. Paul does not hesitate to say—what must have seemed blasphemy to the Jews and is startling even for him—that this was God's intention in the reign of the law. He meant it, by evoking the instinctive antipathy of the flesh, to multiply transgressions, and so to bring man to despair. No doubt it is the Mosaic Law of which Paul says this, both in Rom. 5 and Gal. 3; but that does not make it meaningless for us. The instinctive revolt against the law which imposes its restraint on our nature is not a Jewish but a human experience; and whatever the law be which brings out this characteristic of our nature, it does for us what the Mosaic Law did for Paul, and we understand his experience through our own. For us, as for him, such an experience is God's way of driving us to seek another way of attaining righteousness than by the works of the law. Human nature, as Paul pictures it in its

[1] W. D. Stacey, *The Pauline View of Man*, p. 162.
[2] Cf. C. H. Dodd, *The Meaning of Paul for Today* (1922), p. 61.

5

unredeemed state, seems to have no relation at all with our calling to be sons of God; it leaves us face to face with an apparently insoluble problem.

Emil Brunner uses a most telling illustration in describing the helplessness of human nature under the law: "There are 'moving staircases' in the undergrounds of our great cities which move downward whether one stands still or is walking on them. Whoever happens to stand on these stairs is on the downward move even though he is trying to walk up. The same is true of those who 'live under the law'. To be sure, there are a thousand possibilities here of going up or down, differences which in their place may be quite noticeable. But it alters nothing as to the general direction. It goes down irresistibly towards judgement. Once one stands opposite God on the ground of law—God demands of man that he shall fulfil his command—then the direction is fixed; godlessness is present in spite of every kind of moral or religious exertion." Such a situation provokes the question: Is there any other possibility, no other "ground" on which we are able to stand?[1] The answer to that, of course, is the message of salvation proclaimed by Paul.

THE ORIGIN OF SIN

It is common at this point to ask how Paul thought that man's human nature had become so alienated from God. This is the kind of question to which Paul gives no firm answer, and for the same reason that we can give no answer. We never knew ourselves to be anything else than what we are, and we cannot go out of our nature to scrutinize it in some assumed antecedent condition. In man as he is—and that is man in the only sense in which we know anything about him—there is that which reacts instinctively against the law, that which is

---

[1] E. Brunner, *The Letter to the Romans*, p. 27.

stimulated by the law, into persistent and determined revolt, that which under such a stimulus reveals the exceeding sinfulness of sin. This is what Paul means by "the flesh" and it has simply to be taken as it stands.

The fact that Paul had no clear conception as to the origin of sin is proved by the presence of three different theories in the Epistle to the Romans. It is first suggested that sin entered the world through the first man,[1] but Paul does not say that all men sin because they are physically descended from Adam. "Nowhere, even in verse 19, does Paul teach the direct seminal identity between Adam and his descendants."[2] Later, in the same epistle,[3] the flesh is said to be the seat of sin. By some means the flesh has fallen under the domination of sin. Man's whole nature has thus been perverted and held under the sway of material forces. In other passages[4] there is the suggestion that sin is an objective personal power which may have existed before the Fall, and which entered the world, taking up its abode in man. In addition to these passages we find that in Eph. 2.2, and 6.12, sin is regarded as the work of unseen spiritual forces which hold the "present age" under subjection. The fact is we cannot go back in our own experience to a time when we had no realization of doing wrong. Similarly, we cannot go back in the history of man to a time when sin had not entered and in which there was no trace of antagonism to the law in whatever form it took; as far as history is concerned, it has nothing to say of such a state. Alike in the individual and in the race the moral state has simply to be accepted; questions of origins are hopelessly beyond our reach.

[1] Rom. 5.12–21. 'εφ'ᾧ in verse 12 may be translated either "in whom" that is, all men have sinned in the person of Adam; or by "because", in which case Paul intends us to understand that all men die because they have personally sinned.

[2] Barrett, op. cit., p. 111.

[3] Rom. 7.25; 8.3.

[4] Rom. 5.12,21; 6.16; 7.17.

We may perhaps find most help in the parallelism between "in Adam" and "in Christ" which pervades Pauline thought. Christians are "in Christ" and this means more than that they individually adhere to Christ by personal faith, though it includes this. It also conveys the idea of membership in his Body, the Church. According to Paul the Christian life was always mediated by fellowship in the divine Society, the People of God. So "in Adam" may well convey the idea of membership in an unregenerate humanity.[1] This would suggest that Adam's sin affected his descendants not merely by way of bad example, but by subtle influences of social tradition in all its forms. Such a corporate view of sin as pervading the universe need not be dependent upon ideas associated with Adam.

The point which Paul emphasizes and to which all religious experience bears witness, is that mankind as a whole and not merely individual man has fallen away from the purpose of God. What is important is to recognize the fact of alienation from God. This means, and it is what Paul maintains, that human society is not what God intended it to be, and that our present condition is a libel on human nature as he purposed it. The human race as a whole and every member of it needs not only education and development, but redemption. It cannot save itself, but must be remade or born again.

THE WAY OF SALVATION

A man of deep spiritual insight might have imagined the way in which such a deliverance could be achieved. As he pondered on the whole tragic situation, two possibilities might have presented themselves to him. He could have argued (i) that if the law lost its provocative character—if it ceased to be

---

[1] For the Rabbinic idea of the unity of the world in Adam, see W. D. Davies, *Paul and Rabbinic Judaism*, pp. 54 ff.

merely a demand which stirred man into revolt, and became instead a power which was able to give him life and strength, then deliverance from the slavery of sin might be achieved. Or he could have argued (ii) that if a man's nature was changed—if the "flesh" instead of ruling man's nature and making the law ineffective, if it was itself reduced to impotence then victory over sin could be won.

In the Christian experience of possessing the Spirit both these results are combined. The Spirit is, in a word, a νόμος δυνάμενος ζωοποιῆσαι or, what is the same thing, a δύναμις through which the law passes into act; it is the union of law and power, in which the strife of sin is finally overcome. But this is anticipating what we have yet to discuss. We may at least say at this point that the law as an external thing does come to an end, and its place is taken, and the purpose which it vainly sought to achieve, is secured by the Spirit. But the law does not pass unhonoured. Even in its external and imperfect forms, of which the Mosaic Law is but one example, it represents the will of God for that particular people and at that particular stage of their spiritual education; furthermore, it is the *will of God* which human nature as a whole (in reacting against the law) has opposed.

It is impossible for anyone who realizes this to imagine that God would ignore it. It is impossible to ask that God should dismiss such rebellion without much ado, and to think that sin does not also carry with it wrath and death in the sense in which we have discussed it in this chapter. It is also impossible not to believe that God will find a way of salvation, a way out of the impasse in which human nature finds itself. And between the passing of the law as an external command and the coming of the Spirit there stands the whole body of historical facts centering in the death and resurrection of Jesus Christ. These facts are the conditions of the Spirit's coming; his coming is not direct, but mediated through these historical events, and, normally, through the Society created by those events. The power to live a holy life is not poured into sinful human nature merely on the ground of claiming immediate fellowship with God; it is bestowed upon such a nature in response to faith in Jesus Christ who was crucified and rose again for us men and for our salvation. The righteousness of God is not transmitted into human nature by the vibrations of some spiritual ether stirred into activity by the human will; it is achieved through the sacrifice of Christ upon the Cross and his resurrection from the dead. It is this which we shall now study in all the relations which have been suggested by what we have already said about sin, the flesh, and the law.

4

THE GIFT OF RIGHTEOUSNESS

THE MEANING OF THE RIGHTEOUSNESS OF GOD

OUR exposition of Paul's doctrine of sin, with its correlated ideas of law, wrath, the flesh, and death, enables us to understand the human situation which the gospel is designed to meet. It is not man without qualification to whom it is addressed, but sinful men; men whose sin has the constitutional and tragic character which we have seen. It is such men who are confronted with the problem: How can we be righteous before God? This desire may find expression in many different ways—a sense of frustration, restlessness, despair. Heidegger in his philosophy of *Sein und Zeit* pictures man as seeking to avoid shipwreck in the banality of daily life through the dispersion and dissipation of his energies on things of passing worth.[1] His failure to achieve this leads him to despair. That is one expression of man's unconscious search for the righteousness of God. Bultmann believes that in the midst of such despair there is a possibility of revelation furnished by the repressed but ineradicable knowledge of finitude. The "derelict's" inevitable awareness of his own transitoriness must contain a real, if crude and negative, knowledge of God.[2] The answer to this situation, according to

[1] M. Heidegger, *Sein und Zeit* (1949), pp. 127 ff.
[2] R. Bultmann, *Essays, Philosphical and Theological* (trans. J. C. G. Greig, 1955), pp. 2, 94, 98, 256 ff.

61

Paul, is a *revelation*: there "is revealed a righteousness of God".[1] Here as well as in chapter 1.18, Paul speaks in the present tense. This means that we must not look on the revelation in the gospel only as something which has taken place in the remote past. The revelation does not stop taking place down the ages. No man can hear the gospel without becoming a contemporary to that which happens in it. Whatever the righteousness of God may be in itself it is clear that it is something of which we ourselves may partake. In whatever sense it is God's, there must be a sense in which it also becomes ours. It is we sinners who have to be justified by it, and if it were not available for our justification there would be no gospel in it.

The Apostle expresses this in various ways. The connection between verses 22 and 24 in chapter 3 implies that it is in virtue of this "righteousness of God" revealed in the gospel that we are justified. In chapter 5.17, he speaks of "the abundance of grace and of the *gift* of righteousness". In 2 Cor. 5.21, he argues that the end of all God's reconciling work—the very meaning of Christ's death upon the cross—is that *we* should become the righteousness of God in him. It is an important point, therefore, to begin with, that whatever "the righteousness of God" may be, abstractly considered, it is something which is destined to become ours.

The phrase itself has been interpreted in several different ways and is one which we must examine closely for it is the dominating theme of the Epistle to the Romans.

One school of interpreters assumes that "the righteousness of God" must mean what it bears on its face; the righteousness which belongs to God, which is his essential attribute, an integral element in his nature or character. In this sense, however, a revelation of the righteousness of God would only mean a revelation that God was righteous; and it may well be doubted whether such a revelation would make much impression on the minds of the men whom Paul was thinking

[1] Rom. 3.21.

about. They would look at it no doubt, perhaps be impressed by it, may perhaps have a wishful feeling that it would be "nice" if they could be like that, but it was far beyond their reach.

For this reason it is usually assumed that the revelation of God's righteousness includes in particular a revelation of the fact that this righteousness is not self-contained, but self-communicating; it is God's, but it flows out from God, as it were, and imparts itself to men. Sanday and Headlam, for example,[1] associate God's righteousness with passages in Isaiah which speak of God's righteousness as "going forth"; or, to use the language of these scholars, "as projected from the Divine essence and realizing itself among men".

The religious truth of this understanding of the phrase need not be disputed. It conveys the same lesson as our Lord's word to the young ruler: "there is none good but one, that is, God." All goodness comes from him; in men it is a stream fed from that central fountain. William Temple says that "we cannot too harshly drive this truth into our souls, however eager we may be to trace 'the grace of Jesus Christ' in others, even in atheists. Apart from him I can do nothing."[2] Paul would have been the last man in the world to deny this, but it may fairly be questioned whether the conception is not too vague to meet the necessities of sinful men. However true it may be, something more is needed to pierce the hearts and consciences of men. It seems to us that the righteousness of God must be brought into integral relationship with the Cross of Christ. Sanday and Headlam do indeed hint at this when they say "it seems a necessity that the righteousness of God should be not only inherent but energizing, that it should impress itself as an active force in the world" and add that there is "one single manifestation" of it, "the nature of which

[1] *Romans*, pp. 34 f.
[2] *Readings in St John's Gospel* 2 (1942), pp. 260 f.

it is difficult for us wholly to grasp, in the death of Christ".[1] But the Cross is not merely "one signal manifestation of the righteousness of God"; in so far as "the righteousness of God" constitutes the good news of God to men, it has no meaning whatsoever but that which it has as manifested in the Cross.[2] We may be getting to know God, perhaps, but we are certainly not getting to understand the Apostle, when we provide an indefinite background like this for the glad tidings of "Jesus Christ and him crucified".[3]

Paul's message is something far more specific, far more startling, than the idea that God's righteousness overflows into man, or that God makes us partakers in his own character.[4] The ultimate objection to such an interpretation of "the righteousness of God" is that it does not appreciate the depth of the tragedy of the human situation. To Paul the problem presented to God by the sin of the world is a moral problem of immense difficulty, and it seems to us that this is an attempt to solve it by ignoring the moral difficulties altogether. The righteousness of God is here conceived as acting after the analogy of a physical force.[5] It "goes out", "energizes", "diffuses itself", as the light and heat of the sun, *irrespective of moral conditions*. It is in its nature to do so and it can never do anything else. But in spite of the biblical comparisons of God to the sun and light, moral problems can never be solved by

[1] Op. cit., p. 35.

[2] Cf. G. Schrenk, *Righteousness* (1951), p. 44 (Bible Key Words from Kittel's *TWNT*): "When Paul sees God's act in the Cross, he is conscious with the absolute certainty of faith, that this is the final and effectual revelation of justice and mercy in one."

[3] Cf. Barrett, *Romans*, p. 82, "Only in consequence of a divine invasion of the closed system of human affairs is it possible for men to believe and to be reconciled."

[4] Cf. A. Nygren, *Commentary on Romans*, "The righteousness of God is not a property resident in God, but God's mighty intervention into our existence, which results in a total change in its condition."

[5] Cf. A. Richardson, *An Introduction to the Theology of the New Testament* (1958), pp. 82, 233.

the categories of physics.[1] Paul grapples far more closely with the moral necessities of the case. It is only when "the righteousness of God" is concentrated in Christ crucified that the essential relations of sin, wrath, and death are made clear to men.

\ Another shade of meaning is sometimes extracted from the phrase by reference to the Old Testament. It is pointed out that according to the Old Testament God's righteousness is manifested when he acts as judge, and that when he does so it is always to see "right" done, to vindicate those who are in the right, to establish righteousness on the earth. This can be illustrated principally from the Psalms. For example, Ps. 35.23–8: "Judge me O lord my God, according to thy righteousness: And let them not rejoice over me. . . . Let them shout for joy, and be glad that favour my righteous cause (literally, my righteousness) . . . and my tongue shall talk of thy righteousness and of thy praise all the day long." Here the righteousness of God is that principle in the divine nature in virtue of which God cannot suffer wrong to triumph over right; when his people are wronged, it is in virtue of his righteousness that he vindicates or, as it may be expressed, justifies them. He pleads their cause and puts them in the right before all. Hence the appeals we have in the Old Testament to the righteousness of God, not as something to be dreaded by his people, but as their one sure hope. "In thee, O Lord do I put my trust . . . deliver me in thy righteousness."[2] "Quicken me, O Lord, for thy name's sake: in thy righteousness bring my soul out of trouble."[3] Hence also the use of the word "righteousness" to describe the great acts in which God interposed in his people's cause and maintained their right in the world. "There shall they rehearse the righteousness of

[1] Cf. J. Denney, *The Death of Christ* (1911), p. 119. Revised Edition by R. V. G. Tasker (1950), p. 99.

[2] Ps. 31.1

[3] Ps. 143.11.

the Lord"—the various manifestations of his righteousness—
"the righteousness of his rule in Israel."[1] And hence also the
combination, so frequent in the latter half of the book of
Isaiah, of righteousness and salvation. "My salvation is near
to come, and my righteousness shall not be abolished."[2]

In view of such passages as these it is argued that God's
righteousness is not retributive justice, but essentially gracious.
It is not something to which justice must be done in order that
grace may be free to act; it is itself grace in action for the
vindication or justification of God.

Here again, no one, I imagine, would deny the religious
truth of such a conception. Assuming that it is the people of
God whom we have in mind, and especially God's people
wronged by the world, we can understand that God's righteousness is that to which they would appeal when persecuted.
Like Christ, reviled and insulted, they would commend their
souls and bodies to him who judges righteously[3] and trust in
him to plead their cause. Paul may have had this in mind
when he writes of the persecutions and sufferings endured by
the Thessalonians "as a manifest token of the righteous judgement of God";[4] they speak plainly of the way in which God as
the Righteous Judge must intervene on behalf of the injured
believers and punish their foes. Even where there is no enemy
fighting against the people of God, we find the righteousness
of God spoken of in this way. Wherever the people of God
are found there is a relation between them and God which
involves obligations on both sides, and God's faithfulness to the
covenant he made with his people is called his righteousness.

This faithfulness is revealed most strikingly when his
people have been false to their obligations, and in this case is
closely connected with forgiveness. God does not forsake his

---

[1] Judges 5.11; cf. 1 Sam. 12.7.
[2] Isa. 51.6.
[3] Cf. 1 Pet. 2.23.
[4] 2 Thess. 1.5.

people when they fall away in sin; he fulfils his covenant obligations when his people seem least worthy to be called the children of God. It is on this basis that the Psalmist can cry out: "Deliver me from bloodguiltiness, O God, thou God of my salvation; and my tongue shall sing aloud of thy right-eousness",[1] that is, of God's faithfulness to all that is involved in the promise to be the God of Israel. In like manner John can say that "if we confess our sins, he is faithful and righteous to forgive us our sins",[2] that is, he is true to the obligations involved in his relation to us as Christians. In passages like these a righteousness of God is undoubtedly spoken of which is a gracious thing and which is exhibited in the forgiveness of sins. What we are doubtful about is whether this interpretation can be identified off-hand with "the righteousness of God" as we find it in Paul's letter.

We notice, in the first place, that in every passage to which this line of interpretation appeals, it is always the righteous-ness of God as seen in relation to the *people of God*. God does right by his chosen people, those who are in covenant relation with him, it may be by achieving their deliverance from oppressors—this is salvation in the sense of the Old Testament; it may be in forgiving the sins of which they repent, and which are not in themselves a renunciation of their covenant with him. No doubt the righteousness of God in this sense is also sometimes spoken of as revealed to the world. "The Lord hath made known his salvation: his righteousness hath he openly shewed in the sight of the nations."[3] But this does not mean what Paul means when he speaks of the gospel in terms of a divine righteousness which is made known to all nations for the obedience of faith; it means that God has delivered *his people* from their enemies, and given an unmistakable demonstration on the stage of history of his fidelity to his

[1] Ps. 51.14.
[2] 1 John 1.9.
[3] Ps. 98.2.

covenant. "All the ends of the earth have seen the salvation of our God"[1] means, "have seen the salvation he has wrought *for us*"; "the mercy and the faithfulness" which he has "remembered toward the house of Israel". There is nothing here to suggest that such righteousness was available for those who are not already belonging to the people of God. ·

In spite of the parallelism of language, there is no correspondence of thought with Paul. He does not proclaim his gospel to people who have a *right* to claim that God should do right by them: he preaches to those who are hopelessly wrong before God. Without hope because, so far as they know, they have no reason why they should count on God's faithfulness towards them. Paul is thinking of people who can count on nothing and to whom his gospel must appear as one of unconditioned love. The righteousness which Paul has in mind is neither the vindication of the good when they are wronged, nor the faithfulness of God to his own elect people when they have sinned against him. It is something far more wonderful and profound. It is a righteousness more gracious, more compelling than either of these. It is a righteousness which puts the ungodly in the right before God,[2] and constitutes into a people of God those who were alienated from him.[3] It is a *mighty act of God in Christ* whereby we are delivered from the bondage of sin and the new age ushered in. This righteousness which Paul proclaims is undoubtedly glad tidings for a sinful world and more than meets the feeling of despair which men have who struggle to free themselves from the grip of spiritual frustration. The very fact that this interpretation meets the needs of sinful humanity, is a good reason for accepting it as the right interpretation. It is one of the grounds for saying that Paul's theology is "mission theology".

[1] Ps. 98.3.
[2] Rom. 4.5.
[3] Rom. 3.19.

EXPOSITION OF ROMANS 3.21–6

Having considered some of the interpretations which have been put forward for Paul's phrase "the righteousness of God", it is time for us to examine in more detail the classical passage in Rom. 3.21–6. What we have said already leads us to assume that when Old Testament passages are used in the New Testament they cease *ipso facto* to be Old Testament words and carry with them a New Testament meaning. Parallelism of words does not necessarily mean correspondence in thought. We also take for granted what has already been made clear, namely, that this righteousness, which is at least named after God has God as its source, and that it eventually becomes man's, and that when this happens man is justified— right with God and right in God's judgement.

For the sake of convenience we quote in full the relevant passage, the translation being that of the Revised Standard Version:

> But now the righteousness of God has been manifested apart from the law, although the law and the prophets bear witness to it, (22) the righteousness of God through faith in Jesus Christ for all who believe. For there is no distinction; (23) since all have sinned and fall short of the glory of God, (24) they are justified by his grace as a gift, through the redemption which is in Christ Jesus, (25) whom God put forward as an expiation by his blood, to be received by faith. This was to show God's righteousness, because in his divine forbearance he had passed over former sins; (26) it was to prove at the present time that he himself is righteous and that he justifies him who has faith in Jesus.

We notice, first of all, that the righteousness of God has been manifested "apart from the law". This does not mean that it has no relation to the universal moral laws which determine the relations between God and man; on the contrary, it is part of the Apostle's purpose to prove that the way in which this righteousness comes to men establishes the moral law, so that God in revealing it not only "justifies" the believer in Jesus, but is himself seen to be "just". The Christian Way may be "apart from the law", but it does not annul the law; it sets the law on its feet.[1] It is "apart from the law" in the sense in which a Jew laid stress on his legal "activist" fulfilment of the law, or a Gentile may make a "humanist" claim to fulfil "natural law". The divine righteousness which the gospel proclaims has nothing to do with human achievement. It is "apart from the law" in the sense that for its fulfilment man contributes nothing except the all-important decision for Christ. This involves, as we shall see, being incorporated into Jesus Christ through baptism.[2] But the first step is the act of faith in Christ.

Although it is "apart from the law", "the law and the prophets bear witness to it", that is, the Old Testament as a whole. What is the link between the Old Testament and Paul's conception of the righteousness of God? It is to be found in God's saving purpose. Some of the passages already discussed will be found to contribute to our understanding of this divine purpose, for it is what holds together in unity the different biblical conceptions of righteousness. The punitive aspect of divine righteousness occupies a comparatively small place in the Old Testament. There is the great punitive prophecy of Isa. 5.16 ff and the judicial righteousness of God is linked with his anger in Ps. 7.9,11. But punitive righteousness is most commonly coupled with the idea of delivering the innocent party in any dispute or trouble (Ps. 72.2,4; 94; 11; 103.6; 9.4). In fact we find in passages like Jer. 10.24, God's righteousness counteracting his punitive anger (cf. Ps. 6.1; 38.1). In such cases punishment is merely subsidiary to a further purpose which God pursues because he is righteous. This purpose is the ultimate salvation of his people—a purpose manifested in his righteous acts from the earliest days (Judges 5.11; 1 Sam.

[1] Rom. 3.31.
[2] See Richardson, op. cit., p. 236.

12.7). There are several passages in Deutero-Isaiah where the words translated "righteousness" are best interpreted in the sense of salvation and redemption.[1] For example, in Isa. 46.13, we have "I bring near my deliverance, it is not far off, and my salvation will not tarry" (R.S.V.). In this passage the Hebrew word does not indicate a quality in God, but rather the *action* of God. In the LXX version a different impression would be given to the Greek reader. There the words 'ἤγγισα τὴν δικαιοσύνην μου, suggest that God had made accessible to people a quality inherent in the divine nature. But it is the idea of deliverance, rather than an ethical quality, which we find in this passage as also in Isa. 45.8,23; 51.5,6.

It was the genius of Paul to enlarge the scope of this correlation between the righteousness of God and his saving activity to include all men. It was probably in Paul's mind when he wrote, "I am not ashamed of the gospel, for it is the power of God unto salvation . . . for therein is revealed a righteousness of God" (Rom. 1.16,17).

This, then, is the link between the thought and language of the Old Testament and Paul's understanding of the righteousness of God. The Old Testament reveals the righteousness of God as that which pledges to save—not as though the inherent, abstract righteousness of God necessitates his intervention for the salvation of man, but because God has from the first made himself known as a Saviour; because his whole antecedent dealings with his people which had tended to evoke trustfulness on man's part, were one promise of salvation, and only when that promise was carried out was his righteousness an accomplished fact. It was Paul's contention that in Christ's sacrifice on the Cross the righteousness of God was perfectly revealed and his saving purposes for mankind consummated. The Cross was not an accident in history, but like the Incarnation it happened in the fullness of time, and in

---

[1] See pp. 65 f above.

6

conditions which make clear a definite purpose on the part of God.[1]

At a time when criticism has emphasized the different stages and varying quality of the revelation of the Old Testament, it is important that we should emphasize this unity of purpose that runs throughout the Old and New Testaments. "It is the whole of the biblical drama and the whole of the biblical literature which bears witness to God's revelation of himself in the story of Israel" and especially the "unique redemptive act, prepared for by the unique action of the living God in Israel" and accomplished in Jesus Christ.[2] From first to last the Bible is occupied with the unfolding of the purposes of God. And because Scripture is the only place where we can find the record of the working out of God's plan with such persistency[3] in the face of many vicissitudes, that we believe that inspiration belongs to it in a unique way. It is to this fact that Paul draws our attention when he says that "the law and the prophets" witnessed to the righteousness of God.

Continuing our exegesis of Rom. 3, we find in verse 24 a certain irregularity in the Apostle's grammar,[4] but the connection of his ideas is clear. The sentence beginning "they are justified by his grace as a gift" is virtually an exegesis of verse 22. When sinful·men believe in Jesus Christ, and the divine righteousness manifested in him becomes theirs, this is what happens: they are justified freely by God's grace. There have been long discussions about the meaning of "to justify". Does it mean "to make righteous" or to "treat as righteous"? It seems to me that the best solution is that propounded by Dr Barrett in his commentary on the epistle. "It is far better", he says, "and more in harmony with Paul's teaching as a

[1] Rom. 5.6 "in due season". See Leenhardt, *The Epistle to the Romans*, pp. 135 f.

[2] *The Lambeth Conference* 1958, 2.8.

[3] The very name Israel is properly *yisra-'El*, God persists.

[4] See Sanday and Headlam, op. cit., p. 83.

whole, to suppose that 'to justify' (δικαιοῦν) does mean 'to make righteous', but at the same time to recognize that 'righteous' does not mean 'virtuous', but 'right', 'clear', 'acquitted' in God's court. Justification then means no legal fiction but an act of forgiveness on God's part, described in terms of the proceedings of a law court. Far from being a legal fiction, this is a creative act in the field of human relations."[1]

Though Paul may have had in mind the proceedings of a law court it should be remembered that the two Hebrew words *tsedeq* and *tsedaqah* which lie behind δικαιοσύνη have a wider meaning than strict justice: in the Prophets they mean the response to the claims of humanity which goes beyond legal obligation (cf. Ezek. 18.19,21; Dan. 4.27). For this reason the function of a judge is not so much to apply the strict letter of the law as to be the friend and helper of the defendant (Ps. 82.3). In the Rabbinic writing *Tosephta Sanhedrin* 1.3 the Aramaic word is actually contrasted with the forensic meaning of justice. Although Paul was more accustomed to reading the LXX version of the Old Testament he was also familiar with the Hebrew and his thoughts must have been coloured not by the abstract legal conception of δικαιοσύνη but rather by these Hebrew associations of *tsedeq* and *tsedaqah*, when he wrote of a man being "justified by his grace, as a gift".

Paul cannot speak of the grace which underlies this act of being made right with God without going on to magnify it. That is what he does when he says that we are "justified by his grace as a gift, through the redemption which is in Christ Jesus". It is possible to argue that what the word "redemption" suggests is not so much the cost of the "gift" as the actual fact. Certainly the fact suggested by the word is not to be overlooked. To be justified freely by God's grace is to have our relation to God and our understanding with him

[1] Op. cit., pp. 75 f.

changed. It is no longer determined by such powers as sin, wrath, law, death, but by Christ alone, and our union with him. But whenever we think of redemption as being "in Christ", the cost comes into view. Paul preached no vague and unembodied redemption to sinful men; the divine righteousness which he offered, and which meant this great emancipation from law, sin, and death, he could only offer in Christ crucified, through incorporation into him by faith.

This Christ Jesus through whom comes our justification has been put forward by God "as an expiation by his blood". What does this mean? The word translated "expiation" has been the battleground of many a discussion. Some have regarded it as a technical term for the *kapporeth* or cover of the ark in the Holy of Holies, translated "mercy seat" in Lev. 16.2, etc. Deissmann, however, argued strongly that the word must not be regarded as a substantive but rather as an adjective and that it means "of use for propitiation"[1] and that here it means "propitiatory gift."[2] An increasing number of scholars are inclined to look upon the word as a masculine adjective agreeing with "whom" in a predicative sense,[3] and to translate "means of expiation" (whom God put forward as a means of expiation).

One thing is now clear and that is that the impression sometimes conveyed by the A.V. translation "propitiation" that Paul is thinking of an angry God who has been appeased by the death of Christ is altogether wrong. Such ideas are foreign to Paul's thought about God, and they are not even implied by the language used. Professor C. H. Dodd has shown conclusively in his investigation of the word translated "expiation" or "propitiation", ἱλάσκεσθαι and its cognates that the Septuagint usage of these words has nothing to do

[1] G. A. Deissmann, *Bible Studies*, p. 126, cf. J. H. Moulton and G. Milligan, *The Vocabulary of the Greek Testament* iv, p. 303.

[2] Deissmann, op. cit., pp. 130–3.

[3] Vincent Taylor, *Expository Times*, April 1939, p. 296.

with the placating or propitiating of the Deity.[1] It seems best to translate the word by "expiation", as in the Revised Standard Version, or "means of expiation".

But what do we mean by "expiation"? The word in ordinary English usage still carries with it the idea of making amends for, paying the penalty for, or even seeking to appease. These are also the ideas conveyed by the word "propitiation", and we are trying to avoid this connotation. In Judaism expiation meant removing from man the taint of sin. It was an act of annulment. Moreover, the deeper spiritual insights had led some men at least to regard the forgiveness of God as the only way of expiation, though the elaborate system of sacrifice obscured this insight.[2] If then we carry into our use of the word "expiation" these deeper spiritual concepts, we shall look upon ἱλαστήριον as meaning that God put Christ forward as the very "personification of his grace",[3] the supreme revelation of his love, the ultimate and final declaration of himself as One who forgives on the sole basis of repentance and faith. This is wholly consonant with the thought of Paul and meets the situation which he is trying to tackle. This being so, one wonders whether ἱλαστήριον would not be more appropriately translated "mercy seat", following the example of Luther and Tyndale.[4]

THE SACRIFICE OF CHRIST

The act of God whereby he revealed his righteousness was the Cross of Christ. When Paul speaks of revelation he does not mean an intellectual illumination, nor does he mean that

[1] See C. H. Dodd, *The Bible and the Greeks*, pp. 93–4; *Journal of Theological Studies*, xxxii, pp. 352–60; Cremer, in Kittel's *Theologisches Wörterbuch*.

[2] G. F. Moore, *Judaism in the First Centuries of the Christian Era* (1927), pp. 117, 500 ff.

[3] O. C. Quick, *Doctrines of the Creeds* (1938), p. 79.

[4] Büchsel, *Theologisches Wörterbuch*, iii, p. 321 favours "mercy seat". Cf. Richardson, op. cit., p. 225, and A. Nygren, op. cit., pp. 156 ff.

a veil which had blinded men to some quality in the nature of God has now been drawn aside. God is One who *acts*. The mighty acts of God in the Old Testament, the Crossing of the Red Sea, the deliverance from Captivity in Babylon, show that God is One who intervenes in the affairs of men and demonstrates his power on the plane of history. Similarly, though there is no suggestion of God offering a ransom or a sacrifice of liberation to the devil, Paul, no doubt, looked upon Christ's death on the Cross as a sacrifice on man's behalf and for man's salvation. The sacrifice of Christ, according to Paul, was the complete dedication of himself to God, an obedience even unto death. The sacrifice was not unlike that to which all Christians are called.[1] The uniqueness of Christ's sacrifice lies in its completeness, a completeness which pointed to his relationship with God as the eternal Son; and it is this which distinguishes it from the sacrifices of men. It is a sacrifice which in the deepest sense was from the very heart of God.

On the other hand, the Redeemer must be really man, for he could only save humanity by partaking of its nature and becoming an actual organic member of it. It was Christ's humanity that made it possible for him to identify himself with the race he would redeem. Paul's theology of redemption would not have held together if he could not have taken for granted that the Redeemer made his sacrifice as a man for mankind.

In regarding Christ's death as a sacrifice we have here a reflection of our Lord's own teaching concerning his death. Jesus adopted the title "Son of Man" and added to this the conception of the "Servant of Yahweh". The figure of the servant as depicted in Isa. 53 has redemptive significance. This is clearly indicated by the use of such expressions as "wounded for our transgressions", "bruised for our iniquities", making "his soul an offering for sin", "bearing the

[1] Col. 1.24; 2 Cor. 1.5–7.

sin of many".[1] Moreover, many of our Lord's sayings seem to anticipate that his death would be a sacrifice for sin. Many scholars think that this is true of the famous passage in Mark 10.45: "The Son of Man came not to be ministered unto, but to minister, and to give his life a ransom for many." The reference in this passage to "the many" suggests that it is an echo of Isa. 53.11 f, which expresses the idea of a vicarious and voluntary giving up of life, together with the thought that the sacrifice was in some way connected with sin.

This, however, is denied by Miss M. D. Hooker in her book *Jesus and the Servant*. After a careful examination of all the passages which appear to refer to Isa. 53, she concludes that there is "very little in the Synoptists to support the traditional view that Jesus identified his mission with that of the Servant of the songs: certainly there is nothing which could be accepted as proof for this view".[2] In the present state of New Testament scholarship there is very little that can be called "proved" in the way of interpretation. We must be content with probabilities when trying to arrive at the solution of most problems. And in this case it is very difficult to resist the arguments of J. Jeremias in his article in *Theologisches Wörterbuch zum Neuen Testament*[3] entitled Παῖς Θεοῦ. It is probable that Jesus did foresee his death although we would agree that "the details of the predictions have in several cases been supplied from the Passion-history".[4] Assuming this, there is a strong probability that Jesus found in Isa. 53 an interpretation of the meaning and significance of his death. If we take the following

[1] Isaiah uses the word *āshām*, a technical term from the Hebrew sacrificial vocabulary.

[2] *Jesus and the Servant* (1959), p. 102. C. K. Barrett also thinks that Mark 10.45 has little connection with Isa. 53. He regards it as a creative reinterpretation of Jewish theological thoughts about martydom. See *New Testament Essays: Studies in memory of Thomas Walter Manson* (ed. Higgins), 1959, pp. 1–18.

[3] See also review by Jeremias of Miss Hooker's book in *Journal of Theological Studies* xi, part 1, pp. 140 ff.

[4] W. Manson, *Jesus the Messiah*, pp. 128 ff.

texts, Mark 8.31; 9.12; 10.33,45, we get a fairly clear picture of the Suffering Servant of Isa. 53.[1] These sayings are not likely to have been invented by later writers, for, as Jeremias points out, the tradition is a pre-Hellenistic one. Furthermore, many of the details were not actually fulfilled in the Passion narratives, and so defeat the purpose for which they were presumably incorporated into the Gospels if they did not originate with Jesus. It seems incredible that if Jesus was convinced that he would die in the course of his ministry that he should not have thought out and spoken about the meaning of his death.

This is especially so when we consider our Lord's saying to his disciples at the Last Supper: "Take ye: this is my body . . . this is my blood of the covenant, which is shed for many."[2] His blood will ratify a "new covenant" between God and man, will create once for all the true Israel, a community of men in perfect fellowship with God. Such a community could only be formed where the ruptured relations caused by sin were healed, and in order to achieve this reconciliation, Jesus regarded his death as being "for the remission of sins".

In view of this, we do not think that Paul can be charged with having introduced a thought alien to the intention of Jesus when he spoke of Christ's death as a sacrifice for sin.

RATIONALE OF CHRIST'S SACRIFICE

In attempting to look for a rationale of this act of God in Christ, two theories have been put forward which we must discuss.

There are those who suggest that Christ's sacrifice upon the cross in some way *satisfied* the justice of God.[3] If, as is very

[1] See R. H. Fuller, *The Mission and Achievement of Jesus*, pp. 55 ff.

[2] Mark 14.22 f. The phrase "my blood of the covenant" may go back to Zech. 9.11. Cf. 1 Cor. 11.25. ἡ καινὴ διαθήκη with Jer. 31.31.

[3] See Weinel, *St Paul: The man and his work* (1906), p. 311.

probable, the "righteousness of God" and the "power of God unto salvation" are equivalent in meaning for Paul,[1] the only possible way of viewing God's justice as having been satisfied is to think of the complete demonstration of his righteousness in Christ, that is of his saving grace, as satisfying the eternal longing of his heart to make known his redemptive purpose to men in all its fullness. This, of course, is quite a different kind of satisfaction from that which seeks to limit the exercise of the love of God until his justice has been satisfied. Nor does it exclude the interpretation of this passage which regards the death of Jesus as necessary to demonstrate God's righteous treatment of sin, which had been challenged on the ground that the sins of past generations had apparently been overlooked.[2] This forbearance on the part of God is now seen to be no reflection on his righteousness. Indeed, it is proof of it since it reveals God to those who have spiritual insight as One whose love is willing to wait, a suggestion of the gospel portrait of the father who waits for the son to return, of the shepherd who seeks until he finds. The death of Christ for Paul reveals the measure of God's love. The magnitude of this redeeming action, set over against man's sin, actually reveals God's judgement upon everything that hinders right relations with him. The Cross enables a man to share the divine view of the seriousness of sin, but to share it without despair, indeed to share it with hope. Jesus dies to show us his hatred of sin as well as his love for men.

We have seen that in the complex meaning attached to the phrase "the wrath of God" there is included the breaking of personal relationships between God and the people whom he has made in his own image. That is what causes the deepest sorrow of the Father's heart. We see upon the Cross the utmost revelation of that wrath when the Son of God himself, though

[1] See W. F. Lofthouse, *Expository Times*, July 1939, pp. 441 ff, and compare p. 71 above.
[2] See my *The Meaning of Salvation*, p. 32.

absolutely sinless and holy was caught up into the consequences of sin (cf. 2 Cor. 5.21) and experienced that feeling of separation—"My God, my God, why hast thou forsaken me" (Mark 15.34). There can be no greater revelation of the nature of God's wrath than that which was expressed in the cry of dereliction upon the Cross. By revealing God's wrath in this way the Cross becomes an essential step in the work of our salvation.[1] Nothing could have shown more clearly God's redemptive purpose than by Christ enduring the wrath of God because he chose to identify himself with sinful humanity. It reveals at the same time the measure of God's love for us; it gives us assurance of his desire to forgive and to save.

If we needed any further proof that the Cross of Christ did not remove any obstacle in God's nature before the divine pardon could be pronounced, we have it in the fact that Paul emphasizes reconciliation as being entirely manward. It all proceeds from God. It is God who "shows his love for us in that while we were yet sinners Christ died for us".[2] It is God "who spared not his own Son, but delivered him up for us all". Nothing could be further from the truth than Goguel's contention that the difference between Paul's understanding of God and the teaching of Jesus was that the latter wished for pardon, while according to Paul, God had first to be appeased.[3]

In what sense did Christ die for us? There are those who, while firmly denying that the death of Christ satisfied the demands of divine justice, maintain that Paul thinks of it as being a *substitutionary death*. This perhaps finds its clearest expression in 2 Cor. 5.14,15: "One died for all, therefore all died; and he died for all, that they which live should no longer

---

[1] Cf. F. J. Leenhardt, op. cit., p. 61 n: "The reaction of God to sin (wrath) is not fully known and lived in all its truth except in the light of the cross of Jesus Christ."

[2] Rom. 5.8.

[3] *L'Apôtre Paul et Jésus Christ*, p. 273.

live unto themselves, but unto him who for their sakes died
and rose again." One can hardly doubt that these words bear
a substitutionary meaning.[1] In some sense Christ has taken
man's place. He has died a vicarious death. The clue to the
understanding of this is to be found in the Hebrew concept
of corporate personality.[2] This is clearly stated in Rom.
5.12–21.

According to this passage Adam is looked upon as the head
of the natural or physical race upon whom sin and death came
because of his original disobedience. Whether Paul looked
upon Adam as an historical person it is impossible to say with
certainty. But this passage shows that he recognized a corporate wrongness as belonging to humanity. At the root of this
view lies the Hebrew conception of solidarity according to
which mankind is regarded as a corporate body which acts
and suffers in its representative. The relationship which Adam
bore to mankind on the natural plane was analogous,
according to Paul, to that which the Second Adam bears to
mankind on the spiritual plane. Through the obedience of
this Second Adam the stream of human history has been
reversed and all who by faith unite themselves with Christ
enter into that new stream of righteousness. All who are
justified are united to him in a corporate body of a spiritual
nature; a mystical union between him and all believers has
been established. There is thus an impressive parallel between
the solidarity of the race in sin and death with Adam and the
solidarity of the new humanity in righteousness of life with
Christ. It seems better, therefore, to use the word "representation" in order to describe the work of Christ rather
than the word "substitutionary". In his life and death Christ
has made a full identification of himself with sinful humanity,

[1] R. H. Strachan, 2 *Corinthians* (1935), p. 107.
[2] For the conception of the Messiah as being representative of Israel,
see Edersheim, *The Life and Times of Jesus the Messiah* i, p. 161, and
Strack and Billerbeck, *Kommentar zum N.T. aus Talmud und Midrasch*, i,
pp. 85 f.

and, in so doing, not only supremely represented the love of God to man, but has also represented man to God. This view does not exclude, but rather involves, the idea of human responsibility, since only as men accept what they see in Christ and make it their own do the benefits of the passion become theirs.

This idea of social solidarity and of Christ as the Representative of the whole human race finds an illustration in modern discussions on the relation of the individual to the community. Sir Cyril Hinshelwood in his Presidential address to the Royal Society in 1960[1] said that there is an almost metaphysical principle which rules the communities of electrons and which co-ordinates the lives of separate cells; there is even some mysterious kind of transmission which regulates the flights of certain flocks of birds. In human society the intricate lines of communication are better known and we are coming to realize that the world of men and women is one in a much deeper sense than we had previously thought. These words of the President of the Royal Society are supported by the available evidence in favour of telepathy, there is a psychology of crowds, there are suggestions of intercourse between the living and the dead. Whatever truth there may be in these dimly apprehended modes of spiritual intercourse, there is no doubt whatever that the universe is a *whole* which is pulsating with all manner of forces and influences which largely mould our lives and destinies.

Yet though the corporate nature of society has been demonstrated the value of the individual has not been lessened. Tennyson wondered that Nature should be "so careful of type" and so careless of the individual; but as the process advances that is decreasingly true. There are not a few signs that, instead of the individual existing for the species, the species is coming to exist for the individual. The great move-

1 Printed in the *Listener*, lxiv, No. 1634, p. 82. See also F. W. Dillistone, *The Structure of the Divine Society* (1951), pp. 216 ff.

ments of thought in human society spread from leaders. Nothing will initiate a change in the climate of opinion save the activity of a minority which in the long run has been stimulated by a single individual. The more advanced a civilization becomes the greater is the variety and effectiveness of the individuals. On the other hand, the greater the variety and effectiveness of the individuals, the richer and fuller is the social environment. Thus the community and the individual are held in mutual dependence. The saying that there is no man whose place cannot be filled loses its force in proportion as social bonds become more manifold and intimate, and as individuals gain in specific attainments and in definiteness of character.

This helps us to realize that the very nature of society makes it possible for One to represent the whole and to change the course of human destiny in a fundamental way. Emil Brunner commenting on Rom. 5.12–21 says: "In Jesus Christ the stream of mankind's history as a whole has been guided into a new channel. Previously, and apart from him, the stream of generations rolls ceaselessly towards a terrible end of destruction—the great pictures of the judgement of the world with their flow of human bodies being drawn into the abyss appear before our view. Jesus Christ orders a halt to this stream of death. He alters its course; the stream of death becomes a stream of life; everything that flows into its current is being carried towards the glorious goal of eternal life."[1]

It is through faith that we step into this stream of life, a term which, for Paul, had tremendous significance and content. In it was concentrated all that his own individual response had meant to what God had offered in the life, death, and resurrection of Jesus. And it is to this that we now turn our attention.

[1] *The Letter to the Romans*, p. 44.

5

FAITH AND RIGHTEOUSNESS

THE righteousness of God about which we were thinking in the previous chapter is presented to us as an act of God in Christ which has been performed on our behalf, yet independently of us. It has been achieved in Jesus Christ who was set forth by God as a means of dealing with sin in his blood. It is as objective as the historical presence of Christ in the world. But although the righteousness of God has this objective character, Paul habitually thinks and speaks of it in relation to that act of faith whereby the "righteousness" becomes ours.

Thus, "the righteousness of God", is "through faith in Jesus Christ",[1] righteousness comes or results from faith,[2] it rests on faith,[3] it is of faith.[4] Similarly "man is justified by faith",[5] all, Jews and Gentiles, are justified through faith,[6] God is "the justifier of him that hath faith in Jesus",[7] and to every believer "his faith is reckoned for righteousness".[8] It is noticeable that Paul connects Christian faith with the faith of the Old Testament. In our search, therefore, into what Paul means by faith we must begin with the Old Testament.

[1] Rom. 3.22.
[2] Rom. 9.30.
[3] Phil. 3.9.
[4] Rom. 4.11,13.
[5] Rom. 5.1.
[6] Rom. 3.30; Gal. 2.16; 3.8, 24.
[7] Rom. 3.26.
[8] Rom. 4.5.

FAITH IN THE OLD TESTAMENT

In the Old Testament the word "believe" occurs frequently, and always represents one Hebrew word which has practically the same sense as its English equivalent. The simplest form (*Kal*) of the Hebrew word means to support or carry, as a nurse carries an infant; another form (*Niphal*) means to be supported and thus make firm; and the form *Hiphil*, which takes an indirect object, means literally to lean securely upon. Almost always the word has a personal object, and usually a definite word believed. So Gen. 45.26, when Jacob's sons told him about Joseph, "he believed them not". Their words did not give him any assurance or mental rest. In Ex. 4.1, Moses says to God, "Behold, they will not believe me". But God gives him miraculous attestation "that they may believe . . . that the Lord hath appeared unto thee". We may also compare verses 8 and 9; also verses 30 and 31: "Aaron spake all the words which the Lord had spoken unto Moses, and did the signs in the sight of the people. And the people believed." Similarly, Prov. 14.15, "The simple believeth every word". Sometimes the term is used without any words spoken. So Sam. 27.12, "And Achish believed David, saying, he hath made his people Israel utterly abhor him; therefore he shall be my servant for ever." But here Achish's mind was at rest about David, and about his future action. Judges 11.20 might be rendered, "Sihon believed not Israel to pass through his border". And here in verse 19 we have definite words spoken to Sihon which are given more fully in Num. 21.22. But he did not believe them, and therefore refused Israel a passage.

To believe in God means to "rest" upon the Lord,[1] to love him and hope in him,[2] to confess that our times are in his hands.[3] The believer is kept in perfect peace because his

[1] Ps. 27.14.
[2] Ps. 37.5 f.
[3] Ps. 31.15.

mind is "stayed" on God.[1] He does not "make haste",
does not scurry to and fro, but finds his strength "in quietness
and confidence" and his salvation "in returning and rest".
And what Isaiah calls believing in God is identified by Jeremiah with the true knowledge of him.[2] It is to know God as
"Rock" and "hiding place", as the saving God with whom is
forgiveness.[3] It is likewise knowledge of one's self in one's
human finiteness and sin. It is to know that "the way of man
is not in himself; it is not in man that walketh to direct his
steps".[4] Isaiah's vision of the Holy One of Israel in the Temple
is also a vision of his own and his people's unworthiness.[5] The
contrast between a merely traditional and external knowledge
of God and the insight of true faith is expressed in Job 42 f:
"I had heard of thee by the hearing of the ear: but now mine
eye seeth thee, therefore I abhor myself, and repent in dust
and ashes."

The opposite of faith is not ignorance but unbelief, refusal
to trust God. The unbeliever forgets God and tries to play
providence in his own life. He makes a covenant with death[6]
and puts his trust in horses and chariots instead of the living
God.[7] He cannot distinguish between God and creatures, and
needs to be reminded that "the Egyptians are men and not
God".[8] Unbelief is living without God. It is wrong as faith
is the right attitude of man to his Maker.

We see, therefore, that in the Old Testament the Hebrew
word has practically the same meaning as the English word
believe. Belief means laying hold upon some person or some
word and acting accordingly. The assurance may come from

[1] Isa. 26.3 f.
[2] Jer. 31.31 f.
[3] Cf. Ps. 130.4.
[4] Jer. 10.23.
[5] Isa. 6.5.
[6] Isa. 28.15.
[7] Isa. 31.1
[8] Isa. 31.3.

immediate observation, or as the result of an inference made from cause to effect, or from effect to cause, or upon the testimony of a speaker, or upon an act performed by some one. The result of the assurance leads to the surrender of the whole man to be influenced by that which he is persuaded to be true and worthy of acceptance./Nowhere in the Old Testament is believing thought to be a purely intellectual exercise. Belief in God is personalistic in character; it never moves on the plane of speculation. It places a man in the "I—Thou" relation; it knows only one dimension, the call of God and the response of man. To use a current term, believing in God is always understood "existentially", and it is usually provoked by an historical event.

Paul never suggests that he uses the words *believe* and *belief* in any other than in this Old Testament sense. Faith in Christ is not the exercise of some mysterious faculty which some men possess and others do not possess. It is the action of the whole man and should not be contrasted with the faith which men have in one another or in some cause. The faith whereby a man believes the gospel is the same kind of activity which drives a scientist to self-sacrificing work when he believes in a cure for some bodily disease. Religious faith is distinguished only by the nature of that which is believed. When the contents and authority of God's words and actions rise high above that of any words or actions of men, they naturally create in us a confidence in God far surpassing, in its complete repose and in its practical effects, any confidence we can place in man.

THE FAITH OF ABRAHAM

The nature of religious faith is illustrated, according to Paul, by the faith of Abraham. In Rom. 4.3, Paul quotes the famous words of Gen. 15.6, "Abraham believed in the Lord; and he counted it to him for righteousness." Here the object matter of Abraham's faith is a definite promise spoken and

7

believed, "look now toward heaven, and tell the stars, if thou be able to tell them: and he said unto him, So shall thy seed be". There is also the personal object, namely God, who in that night had spoken these words of promise. Evidently, Abraham's faith, which God reckoned to him for righteousness, was an assurance that God's word would come true. As Paul says, "he believed . . . according to that which was spoken". The doubtful mind was set at rest; the rest was brought about by the action of God, through the instrumentality of the spoken word and accepted as true. God's word gave Abraham assurance, in spite of the apparent physical impossibility of the promise, because of the known power of him who had promised. The process of faith is seen in Rom. 4. 20 and 21, "and being fully assured that, what he had promised, he was also able to perform, wherefore it was also reckoned unto him for righteousness". In other words, God gave Abraham the gift of righteousness because he accepted the assurance which God had given. The promise involved an event contrary to the ordinary course of nature, yet because Abraham recognized the power of God and the faithfulness of God, he was prepared to surrender his whole life to him. He realized that he had no hope for the future except in God, and that for the fullness of life he must trust in God's promise and obey his commands. Faith is, therefore, much more than mere assent to a proposition. It is conceivable that a man should give a bare assent to the existence of God and be uninfluenced by it. But faith as we find it in the Old Testament as a whole, and in the life of Abraham in particular, involves personal surrender to God which leads to a complete change in life.

Such an act on Abraham's part was rational; and its reasonableness is capable of logical statement. To Abraham it was less likely that God should break his word than that the known course of nature should be set aside. Intelligent faith is always a reasonable interpretation of the known facts of the case. In Abraham's case there was, on the one side, the limited knowledge of the workings of nature, and on the other side, the complete assurance in his mind that it was Almighty God who had spoken to him. He did not close his eyes to the facts. Faith does not mean indulging in an optimistic self-deception, nor does it mean adopting the easy idea that things always somehow come out right in the end.[1] Abraham saw the situation as it really was, including, we may say, the possibility that his neighbours would say that God's promise was absurd, or that he had been mistaken. The whole point of Paul's illustration is that in the face of all the difficulties Abraham did not weaken in faith. It was because Abraham did not trust his own powers that he could face the apparent impossibilities of the situation. Faith is the direct opposite of self-reliance, the opposite of confidence in one's own adequacy and resources. Faith is what it is because it depends on the faithfulness of God in contrast to the fickleness of man.[2]

There is nothing irrational in this. If the faith which can best perform the task of making a man's experience coherent with other aspects of reality, is one which recognizes a special revelation of God to man, then that faith is seen to be supremely rational. The really rational act is not one which can be logically demonstrated as true, but the one which, when it is believed as true, makes a coherent sense of our experience. That is what happened in Abraham's case, though it was not until after making the act of faith that it was made apparent that he was justified in doing so.

There is, according to Paul, a precise correspondence between faith as we see it in Abraham and faith in those who believe in Christ. We have in earlier chapters discussed the human situation and the nature of the righteousness revealed by God. The more man struggles in his own power to escape from despair, frustration, and disunity, the more he finds

[1] See A. Nygren, *Commentary on Romans*, pp. 178 ff.
[2] Cf. Isa. 40.6–8; Ps. 36.5–7.

himself involved in the very things from which he would escape. In order to meet this situation, Christ, as the living centre of the race, confessed our sins and acknowledged as one of us, and as our representative, the justice of the divine reaction against sin. His repentance was in a sense vicarious, because he was personally free from sin. It was this, indeed, which enabled Christ to become man's representative by intrinsic right.[1] He could not, in fact, have felt to the full the shame and guilt of our sin if his conscience had been defiled. The link that binds mankind to him is due neither to pious fancy nor to legal fiction. It is essential and it is vital. It rests in the fact that the whole race was "in the beginning created in him".

JUSTIFICATION BY FAITH

That is what God has done in Christ. Justification in the New Testament is not spoken of in terms of human enlightenment, moral reformation, or spiritual growth. It is the creation of a new status achieved by God in Christ. And in order to make that new status our own we must enter into the corporate personality of Christ's body, the Church. That is what Paul means when he speaks of being justified by faith. We need to remember that "the righteousness of God" which Christ made available for us is not some property or moral virtue which belongs to God and which is bestowed on men and so making them holy. When men are justified by faith it means that they share in the verdict of acquittal, enjoy the forgiveness of sins, achieve a new status in God's sight; they are made right with him, through Jesus Christ our Lord. This is the good news or the gospel which Paul proclaimed. When Paul says that the gospel is the power of God unto salvation to everyone who has faith, he is not suggesting that God having done his part in making "righteousness" available for men, it is now up to man to make a worthy contribution

[1] Cf. H. W. Robinson, *Redemption and Revelation* (1942), p. 261.

and win in his own power what God offers. Faith is not a condition which makes salvation possible: it is the power of the Cross which makes it possible for a man to believe, which creates faith in him. As long as the sinner holds on even with his finger tips, as it were, to something for which he claims the initiative or regards the credit as his own, then he does not abandon himself wholly to God, he does not die with Christ and rise again with him to a new life. The very meaning of the gospel is that the sinner is not in the position to meet any conditions which may be laid down by God. The gospel does not demand any assurances, because it is the business of the gospel to create them.

This is in accordance with the teaching of Christ in the gospels. "God is not a task master who loves only righteous men and rewards them in proportion as they have succeeded in keeping his rules."[1] One need only recall the parables of the Forgiving Father,[2] the Pharisee and the Publican,[3] and the Labourers in the Vineyard,[4] to see in Jesus' teaching the picture of God as One who forgives freely and to the uttermost. This is the essence of Paul's teaching that salvation is God's gift, and that the "righteousness of God" becomes man's on the basis of faith.

Even the faith by which we turn to God and accept the gospel is not human faith in the sense that it is worked up in ourselves by the exercise of the will or the stirring up of the emotions. It is created or evoked by God.[5] There have been

---

[1] J. Baillie, *The Place of Jesus Christ in Modern Christianity* (1929), p. 93.

[2] Luke 15.11–24.

[3] Luke 18.9–14.

[4] Matt. 20.1–16.

[5] Eph. 2.8. Cf. C. H. Dodd's comment in *Abingdon Bible Commentary* (1929): "'Saving faith' must not be regarded as a meritorious activity of the human will, but as itself God's gift." The Jews extolled faith as the highest religious achievement, but the very fact that they considered it as an *achievement* shows that they included it under the category of works. Cf. *Mechilta* vii, on Ex. 14.31, Strack and Billerbeck, *Kommentar zum N.T. aus Talmud und Midrasch*, iii, pp. 186 ff.

two main theories in regard to this which must be rejected because they seek to resolve a paradox by logic instead of by experience.

The first one is that which is commonly associated with the continental Reformers of the sixteenth century. Both Luther and Calvin insisted that the bondage of the will of natural man under sin left no room for the exercise of any factor except that of grace. Calvin so completely closed the door to human activity that man appeared as a wholly passive instrument controlled by forces which he could do nothing to help or resist. An instance of this attitude is found in the Canons of Dort. In them it is taught that as a result of their corrupt nature, "all men are thus the children of wrath, incapable of any saving good; without regenerating grace neither able nor willing to return to God, to reform the depravity of their nature, nor to dispose themselves to reformation".[1] According to this doctrine the knowledge of God which belongs to man through the faint light of human nature has no saving value. To stress the truth that faith is God's gift to the neglect of its character as including man's decision is fatal to the dignity of man. It treats man as wax upon whom God places his seal, without evoking any personal challenge.

The other theory which must be rejected is the opposite of the one we have just mentioned. It lays the whole stress on the value of man's human response to the offer of "righteousness". The analogies on which this theory rests are those instances in which the example of one human personality removes out of the way stumbling-blocks which hitherto have remained insuperable. A single hero may, by the stimulus of example, turn a mob into a band of disciplined men like himself. And under that stimulus they can and do perform acts of valour which at an earlier stage appeared quite impossible. The leader lends to his followers his own strength

[1] Session VI, Chapter v. See E. Brunner, *The Christian Doctrine of God* (1949), pp. 322 ff.

and discipline with the result that they become true to their
best nature and are no longer the cowards they were. In the
same way it is said that the moral appeal of the death of Christ
is so overwhelming that no reasonable man can resist it. It
appeals to all that is best in human nature and only the in-
sensate can remain unmoved.[1] Such a theory, in the long run,
appeals to the will through the imagination. The imagination,
however, is a weak and fickle servant, and the mind which
cannot visualize the life and death of Jesus, as an example of
self-sacrificing devotion, must go untouched. If we are to
depend on this for our salvation then our chances are tenuous
indeed.

The paradox remains: the decision which faith makes is a
real choice, yet it is no work of man's. The believer takes his
stand on God's side because he can do no other, yet this act
of his is the expression of his personal freedom. The problem
is how to combine dependence upon God which a God-given
faith implies and the independence which is an essential
quality of a moral person.[2] The New Testament is usually
unconcerned with speculative problems such as this. But it
leaves us no doubt as to where it stands on this particular
issue. Its gospel is a gospel of freedom from the bonds of a
world-order which, so far as it had organized itself apart from
God, meant slavery for all who were caught in its net. When
Paul alludes to the bondage under the elements of the world,[3]
he is thinking of true freedom which consists in getting loose
from an evil world-order which is subject to planetary

[1] For exemplarist theories of the atonement of various kinds see H.
Rashdall, *The Idea of Atonement* (1919) and V. Storr, *The Problem of the
Cross* (1925).

[2] Cf. K. Barth, *Doctrine of the Word of God* (1936), pp. 260 ff, faith is
"man's self-determination in accordance with the determination of his
existence by the Word of God". See also J. A. T. Robinson, *In the End God*
... pp. 110 ff. For the biblical ideas of divine sovereignty and human
freedom, see Quell and Schrenk in *Theologisches Wörterbuch zum Neuen
Testament*, iv, pp. 147 ff.

[3] Gal. 4.3.

revolutions. Paul's answer to that is to point to God's initiative. And the fact is that if we rule out God's grace in breaking the bondage of sin, man becomes more and more the slave to the limitations of his human nature and his environment. The good news of the gospel is not only that the "righteousness of God" is available for men, but also that God provides the means by which man is enabled to respond. Faith is a divine gift which enables us to respond to God's revelation. Dependence and independence are like two circles, never intersecting, yet each enclosing human life and each indispensable. When we begin to think of the matter concretely the whole idea of the delimitation of spheres, of so much being given to man and so much to divine faith, fades away. The point that Paul is trying to get home is that when we do recognize what God has done for us and respond in faith, we should realize that this very recognition and response is evidence of the power of the gospel, and that we already belong to Christ.

That is why Paul can ask, "Where then is the glorying? It is excluded. By what manner of law? of works? Nay; by a law of faith."[1] The implication here is that faith is not a work of the law, there is nothing personally meritorious in it, nothing on the ground of which man may claim acceptance with God as his due.[2] It implies a relation to God into which such ideas cannot intrude. In so far as they do then the response is not complete. When the sinner looks in any other direction than to God's mercy for the origin of his reconciliation with God, he loses the "joy and peace in believing" which are his birthright in Christ. But although boasting is excluded in this sense, it is introduced in another, through faith. By believing Abraham gave glory to God and the man

---

[1] Rom. 3.27.

[2] The fact that different prepositions are used to link the words δικαιοσύνη and πίστις shows that faith is not a special kind of meritorious work. The phrase δικαιοσύνη διὰ τὴν πίστιν never occurs. Cf. G. Schrenk, *Righteousness*, p. 48.

who has been justified by faith also makes his boast of the Lord. "To glorify" is a favourite word of Paul: exultation, triumphant assurance, glorying in God, are the characteristic fruits of the Apostle's faith.[1] He knew better perhaps than anyone else what that word means: the joy of the Lord is your strength.

FAITH UNIVERSAL

This gift of faith is not limited to any one group or race of people. It is the common possession of all men in virtue of the fact that they have been made in the Image of God. The Fall may have defaced the Image of God in man, but it has not destroyed it. The fact of religion is enough to show that fallen man is not ignorant of his Creator, yet it shows, just as plainly, that he does not know him truly. No explanation can be given why some respond to God with this gift of faith and some do not. There is perhaps a partial parallel in the different realm of aesthetic value-judgements, though the moral element there is much less prominent. In both cases we may refer to the influence of training and environment which undoubtedly condition the ultimate attitude. But in neither case do they lead to something inevitable. If we could guarantee the result of universal Christian education, that would be a denial of the very freedom and moral responsibility which is one of the chief prerogatives of human personality. Christian faith is the free response of the human personality to the revelation made by God.

Paul certainly thought that faith was a universal gift of mankind. The inseparable association of "faith" and "all" is very striking in the epistle. The obedience of faith is to be won among all nations;[2] the gospel is the power of God to

[1] Καυχᾶσθαι, Rom. 5.2, 3, 11; Phil. 3.3. See R. Bultmann, *Theologisches Wörterbuch zum Neuen Testament*, iii, p. 648.

[2] Rom. 1.5.

everyone who has faith,[1] to the Jew first, and also the Gentiles;
the righteousness of God is through faith in Christ Jesus, upon
all that believe without distinction;[2] any Christian is ade-
quately described as one who has faith in Jesus.[3] It is in
harmony with this that Paul asks, when he has finished his
exposition of faith and righteousness in their relations to one
another, Is God—that is the God who has been revealed in
Christ's sacrifice—a God of the Jews only?[4] Does that mighty
act of God appeal only to something national, so that only
those born in a certain line, and trained in a certain tradition,
can respond to it? Far from it. That to which the Cross appeals
is neither distinctively Jewish nor Greek, neither ancient nor
modern, neither East nor West: it is simply human, and all
may respond to it by the exercise of faith. Christ is the
representative of all mankind and all have the right to claim
what Christ has won for them. In Rom. 5.15 ff the argument
is that as the one representative of the human race brought
disaster upon *all*[5] men, so by the act of God in Christ, another
representative, the entire species of mankind, may be saved
if each individual embraces the redemption offered to them
by the free grace of God. "Condemnation and justification
are thus both of them universal possibilities, in the sense that
they point to a dialectical truth which is valid for mankind as
a whole, and for each individual man."[6]

Such a faith naturally abolishes all national distinctions;
the only realities that matter are the Father whose love has
been revealed in Christ, and the soul in which the Spirit
creates the response of faith. Paul was conscious of the
universal appeal of the gospel from the very hour of his con-

[1] Rom. 4.16.
[2] Rom. 3.22.
[3] Rom. 3.26.
[4] Rom. 3.29.
[5] "The many" in verse 15 almost means πάντας in verse 12 and
πάντας ἀνθρώπους in verse 18.
[6] Barrett, *Romans*, p. 117.

version: it pleased God, he says, to reveal his Son in me, that
I might preach him among the nations.[1] It was not a Jew as
such who was saved on the road to Damascus, but a man who
was a sinner; and the same appeal, made to the same necessity,
and evoking the same response, was independent of all national
limitations. The Cross, as Paul interprets it, speaks in a language to which faith gives every man the key; if we make
it out at all, we see this, and know this, that there is but one
way in which circumcision and uncircumcision, ancient and
modern, cultured and uncultured, can be made right with
God, and that is by being incorporated into Christ by the act
of faith.

The turning point in history has, therefore, come. It has
come not as new knowledge, a new way of life, a new religion,
or as a system of philosophy or ethics, but by God himself
stepping into the arena of history and radically changing the
status of mankind. The righteousness of God has broken forth,
the life of God himself, the love of God which is the only
absolute right, the right that is divine, has been revealed.
When man trusts in what God has done, no matter who he is,
or what his past experience has been, he becomes a new creation, and may grow to maturity until he reaches the measure
of the stature of Christ.

FAITH AND LAW

It may seem from all this that faith has abolished the law.[2]
In some ways, of course, that is true. In so far as the law means
anything that is national, historical, statutory, it is abolished.
Christ is the end of it to every one who believes;[3] the Jewish
religion is superseded. We are under the law no longer; it is
not a system of precepts and of prohibitions by which our life

[1] Gal. 1.16.
[2] Rom. 3.31.
[3] Rom. 10.4.

is ruled. The life which we live is that which grace calls into being through faith; not restraint but inspiration is the mark of the Christian's life. But where Paul discusses the connection between faith and righteousness, what he is concerned to maintain is that faith does not annul the law, but rather sets it on its feet. What conception of the law is implied here?

It may be plausibly argued, if we look at the sequence of chapters 3 and 4, that what Paul wishes to prove is that the way of being right with God which we discover in the Old Testament, which in a large sense may be called law, is not subverted, but confirmed under the Christian dispensation. In other words, he wished to prove that in all ages men have been justified in the same way—that Abraham, for instance, is the spiritual ancestor of all believers, the type of that attitude to God which has its final and perfect manifestation in Christian faith, because faith is a response to the final and perfect revelation of God. There is truth in this, for as we have seen there is a unity in the Bible which enables Christians to use the Old Testament as an inspired record. In this sense an argument that faith does not annul but confirms the law would find support from our Lord's words, "I came not to destroy but to fulfil".

But if we consider both what precedes (3.21–6) and what comes after (e.g. 8.4), it is clear that what Paul means in 3.31 is something quite different. Law to a Jew, and for that matter to most men, is a symbol of the distinction between right and wrong, even a guarantee of righteousness; and what Paul asserts is that faith is so far from annulling that distinction that it actually establishes it. There were people in the Church at that time who accused Paul of antinomianism, of allowing ethical discipline to give way to unchartered licence. We can imagine his opponents arguing that law is surely the force that keeps sin within bounds. If, therefore, this Paul says that the Christian is "free from sin", and at the same time adds that he is "free from law", and no longer under its dominion, then surely the result will be to give sin free rein. Paul was indignant at the charge and took considerable pains to refute it in Rom. 6.15–22. There is nothing, the Apostle maintains, to which the distinction of right and wrong is so inviolable as faith; there is nothing which shows so clearly that distinction; nothing which is so productive of the good life; nothing which can produce such high moral standards as faith.

Paul could appeal to his doctrine of the Cross. The faith which is charged with subverting the law of God is a faith which has Christ set forth in his blood as its object and inspiration. Now what is the meaning of that object? According to Paul, it is Christ bearing sin, Christ accepting and making his own, as our representative, in all their tragic reality the responsibilities in which sin had involved us. How, then, can the faith which such a Christ evokes but have the moral characteristics of that sacrifice in its very substance? How can it do anything else than treat as absolutely real that righteousness of God to which Christ's sacrifice is the complete homage? Faith begotten by Christ, set forth as an expiation in his blood, is faith to which sin is all that sin is to God, holiness all that holiness is to God; it is so far from perverting morality that in a world of sinful men it is the one guarantee that can be given for a genuinely good life. It is with such an impression of it on his heart that Paul writes: I am not ashamed of the gospel, for it is a divine power to save in the case of every one who has faith; for in it a divine righteousness is revealed of which faith is the very element.

"To believe", to have responded by faith to Christ's sacrifice on the cross, means that we have been incorporated into Christ, so that we live in him and he in us. It is not a case of having an external law that commands us to adopt a certain kind of behaviour. We have the law written in our hearts. This means that it is not a rule outside of us which we have to obey. It would not even be correct to say that through faith there is given to us a power which enables us to keep the law of God.

For the law no longer exists as a set of rules of this kind. It is not we who have to do the law, it is rather that what the law ordains has been fulfilled in us. The Christian lives the will of God and the will of God lives in him. That is what happened when we were justified by faith. The basic motives of life were redirected, the object of our affections was changed. This new relationship having been created, the longer it is maintained by repeated acts of faith, the more spontaneously does the Christian live the good life and the richer grows the cluster of Christian virtues.

But here we find ourselves passing into a different conception of "righteousness". In fact we find Paul using the word in three different ways. There is, first, the righteousness which is demanded by the Mosaic Law.[1] So far as the Christian is concerned this has no claim upon him. There is also the righteousness of God which indicates the act of forgiveness on God's part, the salvation which is the gift of God through Christ.[2] And there is, thirdly, the righteousness which is expected from the Christian in consequence of his death unto sin, of having been transferred from the old creation to the new.[3] Although the righteousness which means the act of salvation, and the righteousness which is ethical conduct are sometimes separated,[4] they are in fact like the two sides of the same coin, and both find expression in the sacrament of Baptism.

[1] Rom. 9.31.
[2] Rom. 10.10.
[3] Rom. 6.19.
[4] Cf. Rom. 5.9,10.

6

RIGHTEOUSNESS AND THE NEW LIFE

JUSTIFICATION AND SALVATION

THROUGH faith in Christ "set forth as a bloody sacrifice as a means of dealing with sin", man is justified. His relation to God is now determined not by sin, or any of the powers or ideas which in Paul's mind form part of the complex of sin, such as law, curse, or death: it is determined completely and exclusively by the act of God in Christ. The man who refuses to make the act of obedience in faith, is in the wrong with God: the man who has achieved a new status through faith in Christ is in the right with God. He is in that relationship to God, in virtue of his incorporation into Christ, which alone answers to the truth as it is in God, as God has revealed that truth in Christ.

Now to be right with God in this sense and to remain right is not a part of the Christian religion, it is the whole of it. The righteousness of God which Paul preached was not merely an element in his gospel, it was the whole essence of it. The justification of the sinner is not a preliminary to something higher; it is not a condition without which real salvation cannot be attained; it is itself salvation. And all other exercises of the spiritual life—prayer, worship, Holy Communion— are subordinate to this; they are to be used in order that the full benefits of that which has already been achieved may be kept fresh and vigorous.

In the mind of Paul the righteousness which is the act of salvation and the righteousness which is the Christian character are inseparable. They are, as we have said, two sides of the same coin. We see this in the following passage from Paul's letter to the Corinthians: "Know ye not that the unrighteous shall not inherit the kingdom of God? Be not deceived: neither fornicators, nor idolaters, nor adulterers, nor effeminate, nor abusers of themselves with men, nor thieves, nor covetous, nor drunkards, nor revilers, nor extortioners, will inherit the kingdom of God. And such were some of you: but ye were washed, but ye were sanctified, but ye were justified in the name of the Lord Jesus Christ, and in the Spirit of our God."[1] In this passage the words "washed", "sanctified", and "justified" are in the aorist tense and express a grace given at a precise moment, at baptism. Baptism thus effects at a single stroke the purification, sanctification, and justification of the sinner. We shall discuss more fully later on the relation between justification and Baptism, at the moment we would point out that there is no suggestion of a gradation of spiritual gifts in this passage. For by placing sanctification between the other two fruits of baptism, Paul shows that it is not posterior to them. The righteousness of the Christian is not merely a potential sanctity, but a sanctity which is already present, the germ of which needs only to fructify. From this we see that justification is not merely a remission of sins; it is a reconciliation with God,[2] who bestows upon us a new status. Hence it is represented as a transformation of our entire being, a metamorphosis, which makes every Christian "a new creature".[3]

This is the point of view from which Paul, in the Epistle to the Romans, enlarges on the life of the justified. In the third chapter he proclaims that Christ is a means of expiation for the sin

[1] 1 Cor. 6.9–11.
[2] Rom. 5.10–11.
[3] 2 Cor. 5.17.

of the world—the revelation of a righteousness in which God's own character is vindicated and in which sinners may become right with him. In the fourth chapter he shows that the way of being right with God is not by meritorious works which claim as a right God's approval, but by unconditional acceptance of what God has done in Christ. This way, he argues, is no new thing, but one which is in principle found in the Old Testament. He points especially to the identity of Abraham's faith with that of the sinner who puts his trust in the living God who can quicken the dead.[1] This is the scriptural way of saying that both are expressions of faith in the omnipotence of God. But in the case of Christian faith this omnipotence has been demonstrated in a way which makes it quite distinctive. It has been revealed in the raising from the dead of One "who was delivered for our trespasses and raised for our justification".[2] In other words, it has been shown in the love of God dealing with the sin of the world. It is not bare omnipotence in which the Christian trusts, but omnipotent grace. In Christ a man comes into contact with the last and highest reality in the universe—God, perfect in love, in righteousness, and in power. And when we say this, we see again how union with Christ by faith is not just a part of the Christian life, but the whole of it. Hence we are not surprised that Paul at this point in his letter brings the whole Christian life into view as the life of the justified, a life which has all its characteristic qualities and virtues present at the precise moment of reconciliation with God in Christ. Holiness is not something added to the act of justification, it is something involved in it.

JUSTIFICATION AND THE CHRISTIAN LIFE

If we use a word from another circle of ideas, and speak of a regenerate life, we may say that justification regenerates, or

[1] Rom. 4.3.
[2] Rom. 4.25.

that faith regenerates. According to the teaching of the Fourth Evangelist in John 3.3–5, the waters of Christian baptism are made potent by the activity of the Holy Spirit so that the new birth may be accomplished in all who believe in Jesus.[1] This new birth involves a new standard of value for, according to the characteristic thought of John, the new realm entered is the realm of truth in contrast to falsehood, of light in contrast to darkness. Similarly, according to Paul, the regenerate life of Rom. 5.1–11 is the life of justification and of faith. It does not matter for our present purposes whether we read ἔχωμεν or ἔχομεν in verse 1, or take καυχώμεθα in verses 2 and 3 as indicative or subjunctive, though in all three cases the indicative seems the more probable:[2] peace with God, access to God, a secure standing in grace, power to glory even in tribulations and to make them subservient to good, and a hope of glory which does not make ashamed because it rests on the assurance of God's love, a love poured out in our hearts through his Spirit—all this is included in the life of the justified. It does not occur to the Apostle to ask, What is the connection between justification and the new life? or, How is the new life mediated to the man who through faith has been justified? These are not real questions for him. The new life as Rom. 5.1–11 exhibits it, is not communicated or evoked as something subsequent to the act of justification. It is the spontaneous manifestation of what justification is and means. It is justification asserting itself as a reality in all the relations, and under all the changing and trying conditions of our time. "We have received the reconciliation",[3] and in that

---

[1] See my *The Religious Thought of St John*, pp. 44 and 188 ff.

[2] W. Sanday and A. C. Headlam, *Romans*, p. 120, prefer the subjunctive, C. K. Barrett, *A Commentary on the Epistle to the Romans*, p. 102, prefers the indicative. In a discussion on Rom. 5.1, J. H. Moulton remarks: "Paul wishes to urge his readers to remember and make full use of a privilege which they *ex hypothesi* possess from the moment of their justification", *Grammar of New Testament Greek*, i (1908), p. 110.

[3] Rom. 5.11.

act of reconciliation we are made a new creation, the centre of our life is changed, and we are exposed to other spiritual forces which enable the newly born child of God to grow to maturity.

It is worth while to notice that this point of view underlies all that Paul has yet to say, and emerges through what might seem at the first glance to be inconsistent with it. To believe in a love of God which is deeper than sin and provides the means of expiation includes everything that the Christian faith stands for. Hence the love of God appears both at the beginnng and at the end of all that Paul has to say about the new life,[1] and in both places it appears in that "wonder" which belongs to it as a love which was revealed in the sacrifice on the Cross. The whole of the Christian life is one indivisible response to this love. It is a love which includes every promise for the present and for the future; it is the basis for all Christian inferences. When we are sure of this love, the love which enables the ungodly to become right with God, much more, says the Apostle, may we be sure that all our other necessities will be cared for by God. If the greater thing, he argues, from God's side is real and true, how much more must the smaller thing too be real and true to us.[2] The greater thing is the wonder of God's love revealed in Christ's sacrifice, a love which is unmerited, unbounded, and inexplicable, by any human standard. The smaller thing is our peace, our reconciliation, our future salvation, and therefore the glory and the praise of our hearts which have been filled with God's love.[3] The same argument is repeated in chapter 8.32, "He that spared not his own Son, but delivered him up for us all, how shall he not also with him freely give us all things?"

But to argue in this way from the love which makes atonement to the other expressions of God's love, such as the provision

---

[1] Rom. 5.5 ff; 8.32 ff.
[2] Rom. 5.9,10.
[3] See K. Barth, *A Shorter Commentary on Romans*, p. 60.

of means of grace to meet other situations, is precisely the
same as to argue that the act of justification in which this
atoning love is received, and in which the sinner becomes right
with God, includes the whole of the Christian life. The new
life is not added to justification; the new life is the immediate
result of that state into which the Christian enters when he is
made righteous, or receives his sentence of absolution.

This interpretation of Paul's teaching on justification may
appear to leave no room for anything in the epistle after
chapter 5.1–11. And indeed the connection between this part
of the epistle and what follows has been the subject of much
controversy. There are those who say that the two sections
must be kept apart—the idea of justification by faith and the
bestowment of the Holy Spirit upon believers are two
separate ideas in the mind of Paul. Others make the connection by the simple process of addition. First, we are justified
by faith—not indeed in the sense of justification explained
above, but in a negative sense, as meaning merely the remission of sins, then we receive the Spirit, as the power of the
new life in baptism; and it is the sum of these things which is
the Christian meaning of salvation. But neither of these views
meets the comprehensive meaning which Paul ascribes to
justification, as including at one and the same time both the
act of forgiveness and incorporation into Christ.

We might be disposed to argue that in chapters 3.9—5.11
Paul is explaining his gospel in its purely religious significance—
remembering, of course, that in a religion which puts a man
right with God, everything is included; then in chapter 5.12–21
he digresses in order to bring out its significance in the spiritual
history of mankind, and particularly to show that the great
figures in that history are Adam and Christ, and its great
ideas, Sin and Grace, Death and Life, as compared with which
Moses and his law have only a subordinate and transient
importance; while in chapters 6—8 the ethical significance is
asserted against possible objections which would find in it an

excuse for sin. But this is to give an exaggerated importance to chapter 5.12–21, which in spite of the important place these verses have occupied in the history of dogma, are hardly more than passing remarks in the epistle.

What is really before the Apostle's mind from chapter 5.12 onwards is the ethical vindication of his gospel. That gospel had been attacked on the ground of reverence for the law, and the main purpose served in his argument by this much disputed passage is to put the law in its place. The law is not what the Jews who slandered him[1] supposed it to be. It is, in fact, a vanishing quantity between Sin and Grace, as Moses is a vanishing personality between Adam and Christ. But after his preliminary discounting of its importance, arguing that the law can only be taken in an historical sense, he comes to face the real objection which was in the minds of his opponents. The law they were concerned about was not to be disparaged on the ground that it was the law of Moses, but because it was to them the law of God. It represented the concern of both God and the Jews for righteousness in man, and their assertion was that Paul's gospel of justification for the ungodly was inconsistent with its claims. It seemed to set no value on righteous living. It only tempted men to say, Let us do evil that good may come, let us continue in sin that grace may abound. If the mere fact that a man was in sin drew upon him the grace of God then he had better continue in sin so that he may also continue to benefit from God's grace! That is the situation to which Paul addresses himself in chapter 6.1 ff.

We see that what is assailed is Paul's doctrine of justification, and that which is assailed is what must be defended. Nothing will serve the Apostle's purpose except a demonstration that justification, as he understands it, is vitally related to the holy will of God, as it is expressed in the law, and to the doing of that will in life. To show that there is something more

[1] Rom. 3.8.

in Christianity than the "righteousness of God" which he has consistently identified with his gospel and to argue that the power needed to create in a man's soul the seed of righteous living was dependent on some other means of grace of which he has yet said nothing would undermine his whole case. That there are other means of grace is clear from Paul's earlier letter to the Corinthians.[1] But these *charismata* are for the purpose of nourishing a man's soul, not in order to create something that is not already present. That has been accomplished in the act of justification. Paul does not mean to imply that his gospel of divine righteousness needs to be supplemented by a reception of the Holy Spirit whereby the Divine life is communicated for the first time. A gospel of justification which has no integral relation with morality, and a new spiritual life which has no vital connection with justification, would be a gospel like Mephibosheth, lame on both its feet.

Paul states the objection of his opponents, apparently in their own words, Shall we continue in sin that grace may abound? Then he exclaims with moral indignation, God forbid! The very idea is shocking. Then—and this is the essential point—he demonstrates its inconsistency with his gospel. This is the meaning of the second verse in the sixth chapter: men who like us died to sin, how shall we continue to live in it? This idea of dying to sin has been in Paul's mind all the time. It is implied in chapter 3.25 ff, where faith is regarded as the act whereby the sinful man abandons himself to the mercy of God in Christ crucified. It is our death that Christ dies for, it is as our Representative that he dies upon the Cross; and when we commit ourselves in faith to the mercy of God which is revealed there we identify ourselves with the act of our Representative, we make that death our own. Sin becomes to us in the very act of believing all that it is to Christ; we are dead to it as he is dead; it is something alien to the new

[1] 1 Cor. 11; 12; 13; 14.

status in which we find ourselves, even as it was foreign to him who died for it. Paul here does not supplement his doctrine of justification, he only brings out its *contents* and shows how adequate they are to answer the objections which have been brought against his teaching on the ground of morality.

Every man, he argues, who knows what it is to be justified by believing in Christ who died for our sins knows *ipso facto* that it involves dying to sin in union with Christ crucified. It is Christ dying for sin who creates faith in a man, and the faith which he creates answers to what he is and what he has done; it is a faith which has a *death* to sin at its very heart. But this is the same faith which justifies, and Paul's argument rests entirely on the fact that it is the same faith. Unless the faith through which the sinner becomes right with God involves in it this death to sin, and, what is not a separate thing, but only the other side of the same faith, a being alive to God, he has no reply to his opponents at all. The same Christ who died also rose again to the new life. And the faith which has death to sin at its heart, has also *resurrection* as its living impulse.

This teaching was no abstract theory in the mind of Paul: it arose out of his own experience. The same experience in which he became right with God in Christ—that is, the experience of faith—is an experience in which he became a dead man, as far as sin was concerned, and a living man, so far as God was concerned. Not that this is the ground on which he finds acceptance with God, or in view of which God justifies him; nothing could be so direct a contradiction of Pauline theology as to suppose that God justifies us because the germ of sanctification or of new life is already present in the soul and can be counted on to develop. It is the one unconditional mercy of God in Christ crucified which creates the one response of faith—a faith in which, as one indivisible experience, the believing sinner becomes right with God and dead to sin. The righteousness of God as the forgiveness of

sins, and the righteousness of God which is right behaviour
are included in the one act of justification.

JUSTIFICATION AND BAPTISM

The whole answer of Paul to the charge that his gospel was
unethical is contained in that exclamation—*men like us who
died to sin!* As we have already insisted, this is no answer
unless the dying to sin is necessarily involved in that very act
of believing in which a man is made right with God. This is
something of which every Christian should be aware, for it
all happened at the moment of baptism.[1] It is not doubted
that in the days of the New Testament all who became Christians were baptized. In chapter 6.3, Paul appeals to what was
apparently common knowledge among Christians, "Are ye
ignorant", he asks," that all we who were baptized into Christ
Jesus were baptized into his death?"

This is something far more than a symbolic or dramatic
act. In the words of Anders Nygren: "When he who is baptized is immersed in the water, the act signifies burial 'with
Christ'; and when he again comes up out of the water, that
signifies resurrection 'with Christ'. But it would be an utter
misinterpretation if, for that reason, one were to characterize
Paul's view of baptism as 'symbolical', in the sense in which
that word is generally used. For, according to Paul, in baptism
we have to do with realities, not merely with symbolical
representations. That which baptism symbolizes also actually
happens, and precisely through baptism."[2] This linking together
of baptism and the Lord's burial and resurrection goes back
to the Synoptic Gospels. In Mark 10.39 and Luke 12.50 it is
implied that Jesus comes not with water only, but with water

[1] The importance of baptism cannot be better expressed than in the
following words of O. Cullmann, *Baptism in the New Testament* (1950),
p. 22; "The temporal centre of all history, the death and resurrection of
Christ, is also the centre of the history of baptism."

[2] Nygren, op. cit., p. 233.

and blood, thus linking the idea of baptism with that of death. In John 1.29–32, the One upon whom the Dove descended at the moment of baptism is described as the Lamb of God which taketh away the sin of the world. Furthermore, according to the Fourth Evangelist, it is when Christ is liberated in death that the Holy Spirit is bestowed upon all who believe. The Spirit was "not yet" because Jesus was not yet glorified. The baptism of Jesus looks forward to the events of the passion and resurrection and the coming of the Holy Spirit.

So far as the teaching of Paul is concerned, when a man was baptized that was the occasion of his justification, his entry into a new status before God. As circumcision was given to Abraham as "a seal of the righteousness of faith", so baptism has been given to the Church by Christ as the occasion when we were "sealed" with the Holy Spirit of promise.[1] It was the moment when we were incorporated into Christ, we were baptized "into Christ",[2] and even as we were united with him in his death, so also we were united with him in his resurrection. This means that we died to the life of the "old world" and were received into the "New Age". As Paul wrote to the Christians at Corinth, "Wherefore if any man is in Christ, he is a new creature: the old things are passed away; behold they are become new."[3] There is therefore good reason to suppose that when Paul wrote about "justification by faith", his readers would understand by this "justification by faith and baptism, or, more simply, baptismal justification".[4] At least if they were ignorant of this meaning of baptism before Paul wrote to them, this letter would quickly put them right!

[1] Eph. 1.13.
[2] Rom. 6.3.
[3] 2 Cor. 5.17.
[4] See A. Richardson, *An Introduction to the Theology of the New Testament* p. 238. Cf. the following statement by O. Michel, *Kommentar z. Römerbrief* (1955), p. 140, "Justification and baptism condition and secure each other mutually."

POST-BAPTISMAL SIN

The theological vindication of Paul's gospel was completed
by this exposition of the meaning involved in the sacrament of
baptism. He knew in his own experience that justification by
faith meant death unto sin and a new birth unto righteousness.
But the theological defence of his gospel and his own experience, raises practical questions which cannot be overlooked. Did Paul, for example, mean by the death unto sin,
that a man after baptism remained innocent? When he says
that a man who is "in Christ" is free from sin,[1] does he wish
us to understand that the reward of becoming a Christian is
perfection? There have been at least two answers to this problem, and we shall look at them in turn.

It is claimed that Paul's teaching does imply that a man is
free from sin in a moralistic way after baptismal justification.
Such, at least, is the theological implication of what he says,
and the very fact, it is claimed, that it is not true in practice
shows the weakness of his theology and, incidentally, of the
Catholic doctrine of Baptism. We shall see presently that Paul
is not so weak in theology as this argument suggests. At the
moment we need only say that it would reveal an extraordinary
lack of integrity on the part of a man who was aware of the kind
of behaviour that existed among the baptized people at Corinth
to assert in his letter to the Roman Christians that they will
always be free from sin as the result of their incorporation
into Christ at their Baptism. It is to be observed that John
makes the same kind of claim in his epistle. In 1 John 3.9,
it is stated that "whosoever is begotten of God doeth no
sin, because his seed abideth in him: and he cannot sin,
because he is begotten of God". Yet the same writer says in
chapter 2.1,2, "My little children, these things write I unto
you, that ye may not sin. And if any man sin we have an
Advocate with the Father, Jesus Christ the righteous: and he

[1] Rom. 6.18.

is the propitiation for our sins; and not for ours only, but also for the whole world." This appears at first to be as sharp a contradiction as we find in Paul. In the first passage, however, the verbs are in the present and imperfect tenses, which indicate that the author had in mind a continuous sinful state. Whereas in the second passage quoted, the tenses are in the aorist and indicate occasional acts of sin. The same distinction is made in John 13.10, where our Lord says to Peter and the other disciples, "He that is bathed needeth not save to wash his feet, but is clean every whit." The reference here is probably to baptism and means that at the moment of baptism a man is cleansed perfectly and for ever; there is no need for a second radical cleansing, but only a washing of the feet from such contamination as is inevitable to all who walk in the world.[1] It is probable, therefore, that Paul had the same distinction in mind when he speaks of the man who has enjoyed baptismal justification as being indeed free from sin in this radical sense. Sin has no more dominion over him for Christ is his Lord. A Christian ought not to sin, he should fight against sin and so witness to his new status. "*Reckon yourselves*", he says, "to be dead unto sin, but alive unto God in Christ Jesus." Remember your new status, be yourselves and every mouth which reproaches the gospel shall be stopped. The implication is that if the baptized Christian should sin it cannot be in such a way that his new status should be completely lost even as the image of God was never wholly destroyed by sin. In the words of Karl Barth, he is "the bearer of a *character indelebilis*".[2]

If he should sin there is always the present advocacy of Jesus, for though his sacrifice was made once and for all his priesthood is perpetual and eternal.[3] The once-for-all character of being justified in baptism is what distinguishes baptism

[1] See my *The Religious Thought of St John*, p. 173.
[2] K. Barth, *The Teaching of the Church Regarding Baptism* (1948), p. 63.
[3] See my *The Meaning of Salvation*, p. 50.

from Holy Communion, while the participation in the death and resurrection of Christ is what connects them.[1] In the Eucharist the Church "shows forth" the death and resurrection of Christ and it is the constituted *community* which repeats the Eucharist day by day. In this service the ἀνάμνησις is not a mere remembrance of past events. It means the continued recapitulation and re-living of the death and resurrection of Christ. But baptism which was the means by which the *individual* was admitted into the redeemed community cannot be repeated as it would be beside the point. Furthermore, our Lord has given authority to his Church to forgive sins: "Receive ye the Holy Ghost: whosoever sins ye remit, they are remitted unto them; and whosoever sins ye retain, they are retained."[2] In these ways the benefits of Christ's sacrifice are made available to all who had been baptized and later committed sins.

Paul's emphasis in the Epistle to the Romans is on the actual moment when a man becomes dead unto sin and is incorporated into the Body of Christ. And this doubtless explains why Paul does not mention the Lord's Supper in this epistle. He is thinking chiefly of Church membership at the moment of its genesis rather than in its subsequent life.[3] It is in 1 Corinthians 11 that he speaks of the Eucharist as the perpetual "showing forth" of Christ's death implying that the benefits of the cross are always available to men in this sacrament. And nowhere does he deny what his fellow apostle makes quite clear, that if we sin after being baptized we have an Advocate with the Father.

The second answer may be made in some words used by Dr C. K. Barrett in his commentary. "When Paul says that 'in Christ' men are dead to sin and alive to God, this is

---

[1] Cullmann, op. cit., pp. 29 ff. In John 13.1 ff the baptismal symbolism of the feetwashing is linked with the Last Supper.

[2] John 20.22,23.

[3] See F. J. Leenhardt, *The Epistle to the Romans*, p. 22.

sacramentally and eschatologically true."[1] It is sacramentally true because at the moment of baptism a man is cleansed of all his sins, his soul is white and pure. In the present age and circumstance, however, such a state of innocence is not likely to last long. And though a man may never lose his newly bestowed birthright, individual acts of sin may never be far away. The manner in which these can be dealt with has already been seen. But as he is already in the "New Age" he may look forward to the time when the promise will be fulfilled and the occasional acts of sin will belong wholly to the past. Righteousness is something which we actually possess in virtue of our new status, but it is also something for which we must wait until Christ shall bring the present "age" to a close and "sum up" all things in himself. What is true of the death unto sin is also true of the resurrection to life. In baptism we share in the resurrection of Christ but we also look forward to the resurrection in the last day. The part which the Holy Spirit has to play as the pledge (ἀρραβών) of the fulfilment of the ultimate purpose of God will be discussed in the next chapter.[2]

THE MEANING OF BEING "IN CHRIST"

What does Paul mean when he speaks of being "in Christ"? Deissmann maintains what is sometimes called the "local view", that is, the preposition "in" is taken very literally, and Paul is said to believe that the Christian is "in Christ" in a sense analogous to that in which we are in the air we breathe, and that the air is in us.[3] This means that Christ is in the believer as an ethereal substance, a life element; and his

[1] Op. cit., p. 127. Cf. Richardson, op. cit., p. 237.
[2] Cf. G. W. H. Lampe, *The Seal of the Spirit* (1951): "The Pauline conception of the Spirit, and hence of Baptism, is always eschatological." See pp. 132 ff below.
[3] G. A. Deissmann, *Paul, A Study in Social and Religious History* (1926), pp. 135 ff.

union with Christ is, if the analogy may be allowed, a mixture of two gases or fluids, something in the nature of a semiphysical process. So intimate and close is Christ to Paul and Paul to Christ, that Deissmann conceives the experience to mean that Christ is "about him on all sides", filling him, speaking to him, in him, and through him, as a present and powerful reality.

There are those who disagree with Deissmann in this interpretation. Morgan, for example, considers it highly doubtful whether the phrase being "in Christ" ever carries the "local meaning".[1] He thinks that no one definite meaning can be assigned to it, but that it is used now to describe one relationship and now another. Its use commended itself to Paul, he thinks, because of its elasticity. It cannot be described or defined in purely ethical terms, but it does indicate a relation of the "closest union and absolute dependence".

This scholar, so far as his general conclusions are concerned, does not seem to grasp accurately the meaning of Paul when he used the phrase, "baptized into Christ Jesus" in Rom. 6.3. He does not put sufficient emphasis on the significance of Paul's teaching about the first and second Adams as representing respectively the old and new humanities. In Rom. 5.14–15 we have a marked emphasis on the idea of Christ being the Representative Man over against the first Adam and in 5.16–21 there is an impressive parallel between the solidarity of the race in sin and death with Adam and the solidarity of the new humanity in righteousness and life in Christ. Those who are united with him become members of that new humanity. This, as we have seen, is what happens when a man is "justified", he is reconciled to God in Christ and becomes a partaker of the blessings of the "New Age". It is in this idea of the Representative Man that we have a clue which enables us to understand what Paul means by being "baptized into Christ Jesus". This is not the language of mysticism for it is

[1] W. Morgan, *The Religion and Theology of Paul* (1917), p. 118.

by faith that a man is incorporated[1] into Christ, irrespective of any mystical experiences. Paul regards Christ as the Inclusive Representative of the New Humanity, so that to be baptized into Christ means to be "plunged" by baptism into him.

The word βαπτίζειν does not necessarily mean to plunge or to immerse, but the context in which the word is found often demands that it should be understood in this way. In Rom. 6.3 the consequence of baptism in Christ is that we are *buried* with him in his death, so that as Christ is risen from the dead by the glory of the Father, so we may also walk in the newness of life. In Gal. 3.27,28, baptism in Christ has two results: the first is to *clothe* us with Christ; the second is to unify us *in* Christ. This is only intelligible if Christ is considered as an element which envelopes us. In 1 Cor. 12.13, the same idea is found, though the form of expression is different. Here the suggestion is that we are baptized into the mystical body of Christ.

To be baptized "into Christ", then, means to be incorporated into Christ. We are brought into union with his death, his burial, and his resurrection.[2] This does not mean that Christ's death and resurrection are reproduced in the Christian. This would suggest a perfection of obedience which can only be ascribed to Christ.[3] It is better to say with C. H. Dodd that it means that the Christian dies and rises again *in solidarity* with Christ.[4] It is thus that Christ provides the means whereby all men can enter into their New Heritage. But if Christians are justified in Christ, they are also justified in the Spirit, and it is to the work of the Holy Spirit in man's salvation that we must now turn our attention.

[1] Cf. W. Sanday and A. C. Headlam, *Romans*, p. 156: "The act of Baptism was an act of incorporation with Christ."
[2] Rom. 6.3,4,5.
[3] See p. 136 below.
[4] See E. Best, *One Body in Christ* (1955), p. 46.

7

THE NEW LIFE AND
THE HOLY SPIRIT

THE SPIRIT OF CHRIST

THE conception of the Holy Spirit is one of the most difficult parts of Paul's teaching to grasp clearly. This is partly due to the fact that the word is used sometimes in the more popular sense and at others in a more specific, one might almost say, technical, sense. It is partly due, also, to its meaning being determined at times by Old Testament associations, at other times by the ecstatic accompaniments of early Christian worship, and even by Hellenistic or semi-philosophic ideas. There are passages where the Spirit seems to possess a physical mode of expression, and others where it has a purely ethical connotation.[1]

But all these difficulties and many others may be covered if we are bold enough to say that for Paul the Holy Spirit is in the last resort co-extensive with Christianity. It is one of the ways in which anything and everything Christian can be described—all such things as are done by a man who is in the Spirit, or who is led by the Spirit, or who walks after the Spirit. To describe the activities of the Christian in this way is to indicate their source and inspiration in God. Of course

[1] For the sources from which Paul drew ideas of the Spirit which influenced his own conception, see R. Birch Hoyle, *The Holy Spirit in St Paul* (1927), pp. 175 ff.

God in this case is not thought of in an abstract way; the God whose Spirit is the explanation of all things Christian is the God who has been manifested for our salvation in Jesus Christ, so the Spirit which empowers all Christian activities is the Spirit of Christ. In a passage like Rom. 8.9–11, Paul speaks of both the Spirit of God and the Spirit of Christ, meaning the same Person. There is, furthermore, scarcely one spiritual blessing or activity which is not at one time ascribed to Christ and, at another, to the Spirit. Christians are justified "in Christ"[1] and "in the Spirit";[2] sanctified, sealed, and circumcised in both.[3] Believers have joy, faith, love, and fellowship both "in Christ" and "in the Spirit".[4] Sometimes Christ is said to be the principle of the new life, and at other times the Spirit.[5] In one place Christ is held to be the quickening power, in another the Spirit.[6] Christ is in the believer and the Spirit is in the believer; both are said to be the assurance of eternal life.[7]

This suggests that Paul identified Christ with the Holy Spirit. In 2 Cor. 3.17, for example, we read: "Now the Lord is the Spirit: and where the Spirit of the Lord is, there is liberty." Before committing ourselves, however, to the theory of identification, we should notice that in this passage Paul is not dealing with the Person of Christ, but rather with the nature of the two covenants: the first, the letter of the law, given by Moses; the second, the covenant inaugurated by Christ who gave the living Spirit. He is drawing a contrast between the legalistic religion of the Jews and the religion of the new righteousness, which is a religion of the Spirit. The former

[1] Gal. 2.17.
[2] 1 Cor. 6.11.
[3] 1 Cor. 1.2; Rom. 15.16; Eph. 1.13; 4.30; Col. 2.11; Rom. 2.29.
[4] Phil. 3.1; Rom. 14.17; Gal. 3.26; 1 Cor. 12.9; Rom. 8.39; Col. 1.8; 1 Cor. 1.9; 2 Cor. 13.14.
[5] Gal. 2.20; 5.16–22.
[6] 2 Cor. 4.14; Rom. 8.11.
[7] 2 Cor. 1.22; Col. 1.27.

9

obeys an external code; the latter springs spontaneously from within. The key word in this passage is "freedom", for Paul is seeking to convey the meaning of the new righteousness which is by faith. It means having a new spirit, the spirit of the Lord. And just as Moses (the old covenant) meant code or letter, so the Lord (the new covenant) means the spirit. The one was tyrannous bondage; the other "the glorious liberty of the children of God". We conclude, therefore, that since the contrast between "letter" and "spirit" is the key to the interpretation of this passage, the attempt to infer from it the identification of Christ with the Spirit of God, is a mistaken one. This conclusion applies with equal force to two other passages which are alleged to support the theory of identification.[1]

If a metaphysical identity of Christ and the Holy Spirit cannot be maintained, there is nevertheless such a remarkable blending of the two in the mind of Paul, that we might speak of a functional or practical identification. In the light of the salvation effected by God through Christ, and the richness of the Christian's experience, Paul found no difficulty in passing from Christ to the Spirit of Christ, and to the Spirit of God, and using them interchangeably to describe what had happened and was continuing to happen, in the life of the believer. On the one hand, the fruits of the Spirit reflect all the virtues of Christ, and, on the other hand, it is only by the revelation that the Spirit imparts that a man can say that Jesus is Lord.[2]

THE HOLY SPIRIT AND FAITH

Just as everything Christian can be defined in terms of Spirit, so everything Christian can be defined in terms of faith, when it is referred to man's response to God as its condition. It is natural when we think of man's responsibility

[1] 1 Cor. 6.17 and 15.45.
[2] 1 Cor. 12.3.

before God to put faith in the forefront, and to make the reception of the Spirit depend upon faith. On the other hand, it is through the Spirit that the love of God which has been revealed in Christ crucified is poured into our hearts, and to that love faith is the only response. Hence it is hardly real to argue about the relations of faith and the Spirit. They are alternative ways of describing the Christian experience,[1] according as we regard them as being expressed through the abandonment of self to God, or the gracious operation of God on and in the soul of man. Faith itself is the gift of the Spirit and the Spirit's gifts cannot be separated from the Spirit himself. In the Epistle to the Romans Paul gives primacy to faith in speaking of justification, probably because at the initial stage of Christianity the emphasis has to be laid on the sinner's refusing or accepting, by a free act of his own, the proper relation to God. It is one way of meeting the paradox which we discussed earlier on the respective activities of man and God in the work of redemption. When the life which follows upon the acceptance of Christ is thought of, primacy is given to the Holy Spirit, probably because the believer is then aware that all his experiences originate in God.

THE ACTIVITY OF THE HOLY SPIRIT

So far in this study the emphasis has been upon faith, but having now considered the act whereby a man is brought into union with Christ in his death and resurrection and has achieved a new status before God, we are able to examine more carefully the activity of the Holy Spirit as it is expressed in this epistle.

In chapter 5.5, Paul says: "The love of God has been poured out in our hearts through the Holy Ghost which was given

---

[1] Cf. J. Denney, *The Death of Christ* (1911), p. 139: "Theologically the Spirit is the divine correlative of faith." Revised edition by R. V. G. Tasker (1950), p. 112. Cf. R. Birch Hoyle, op. cit., pp. 124 f.

unto us."[1] The aorist tense here no doubt indicates that the Spirit was bestowed at a definite moment in the past, probably when the Christian was baptized. The experience at the moment of Christian initiation which is ascribed to the Holy Spirit is the assured consciousness of God's love which enables the new-born Christian to endure tribulation. It is of God that we have such a conviction as this; he has wrought it in us by his Holy Spirit; we could never have attained it otherwise. The love of God which is poured into the heart of the Christian like refreshing water on parched ground is the love which was manifested in Christ's death for sinners; it is in making this live in our hearts, and in enabling us to realize that it is ours, that the Spirit reveals his presence in our souls. The Spirit, then, does not speak of himself, but witnesses to the love of Christ which dwells in us. Through his witness in our souls we perceive the presence of Christ.[2]

This is precisely the teaching of the Fourth Evangelist. In St John's gospel the Holy Spirit is regarded as the abiding representative of Christ, in whom he himself returns to his disciples.[3] The Holy Spirit is the witness to Christ[4] and calls to remembrance his words,[5] and takes of the things of Christ and declares them to his disciples.[6] In the First Epistle of St John the gift of the "unction" enables the disciples to dwell in Christ.[7] The witness of the Spirit is so complete that Jesus himself is present wherever the Spirit is. The coming of the Spirit is also the advent of Jesus.

One might have thought that Paul would have introduced the Holy Spirit into the theological interpretation of history

---

[1] ἐκχέω = to pour out. Cf. Isa. 44.30; Joel 2.27,28.

[2] There is a good discussion on Rom. 5.1-11 in L. S. Thornton, *The Common Life in the Body of Christ* (1946), pp. 78 ff. He regards it as the fullest statement about justification in the Pauline epistles.

[3] See my *The Religious Thought of St John*, p. 211.

[4] John 15.26.

[5] John 14.26.

[6] John 16.14.

[7] I John 2.27.

which he gives us in the parallel between Adam and Christ. The reason for the omission is perhaps due to the speculative nature of what he says. The Apostle's intellect is stirred by the vast conceptions of the unity of the race in sin and in redemption, in Adam and in Christ. It is certainly his own personal experience, and still more his own hope, which turns the parallel into a contrast, and annuls the reign of sin in the surpassing glory of the reign of grace. But in spite of this foundation in experience, and this personal assurance, there is something in this passage which is speculative, and the want of any reference to the Spirit may have been due to Paul's awareness of this.

What is surprising is the absence of any mention of the Holy Spirit in chapter 6. It may indeed be asked whether Paul did not assume the presence of the Spirit as being necessarily involved in baptism. The connection between baptism and the Holy Spirit is normal throughout the New Testament and Paul himself elsewhere links the experience of conversion, baptism, and the Holy Spirit together.[1] Yet there is a reason why the Spirit should not be mentioned in connection with baptism at this point in his argument. When Paul refers to baptism he is not so much thinking of the action of the Spirit, though it is no doubt present, as trying to draw out what is involved in faith. The idea underlying all he says is not that baptism brings the gift of the Spirit, and so of a divine life which expels sin, but that in baptism there is re-enacted the truth that the faith which is declared in it involves a death unto sin, with which continued life in sin is incompatible. Paul refrains from speaking of the Spirit in this connection because in the first instance he is thinking not of death unto sin from the point of view of Christian privilege, but from that of Christian responsibility. The death unto sin is involved in faith, the great free act of surrender to the sin-bearing love of God in Christ crucified. To take this act

[1] Gal. 3.1,2; 1 Cor. 6.11,12,13.

seriously involves the new life of righteousness as we have seen. No doubt Paul could have expressed himself differently and explained the Christian's freedom from sin as being due to the creative act of the Holy Spirit in union with Christ's death and resurrection. This merely shows that Paul has various ways of interpreting the same experience. The focus of the variety is Christ, for both faith and the Holy Spirit are related to Christ. The faith which abandons itself to Christ involves receiving the Spirit of Christ. Where human responsibility is to be emphasized, it is naturally faith which is put to the front; where the action of God is the main point, prominence is given to the Spirit. But whether we speak of faith or the Holy Spirit in this connection, we say something that derives its whole meaning from Christ.

It is this essential relation of the Holy Spirit to Christ and the Father which explains the fact that in almost every passage where the Spirit is mentioned, there is a contrast expressed or implied to some condition or experience which is purely human. The nature of the Spirit has always to be defined by contrast. The Spirit is power as opposed to weakness, freedom as opposed to bondage, adoption as opposed to slavery, holiness as opposed to the flesh of sin, life as opposed to death. The very fact that the work of the Holy Spirit is co-extensive with Christian experience makes it impossible to give any systematic treatment of the subject in narrow limits. The following survey of the relevant passages in Romans may serve to bring out the function of the Holy Spirit in the present life of the Christian and in providing a pledge for the future triumph over evil.

The first is chapter 7.6: "We serve in newness of the spirit, not in oldness of the letter." The newness or freshness which is characteristic of Christian service is due to the presence of the Holy Spirit. It is because he possesses the Spirit that the Christian does not find the service of God grow stale or formal. When religion is regarded in terms of law, of the "letter", then worship, prayer, and service sink into the heavy routine of custom, or into a punctilious and scrupulous conformity to details in which the spontaneity and life have gone. But religion of the Spirit is characterized above all else by zest and freshness. "The kingdom of God . . . is righteousness and peace and joy in the Holy Spirit."[1] The Christian is one who rejoices in hope.[2] He knows that the great victory over sin has been won. God has shown that love is stronger than hate, and that life is stronger than death. He knows that he has been made a partaker of that victory and the possession of the Spirit is the pledge that one day history will come to an end and God's kingdom of righteousness alone remain. God's world, even in the present, becomes suddenly full of new ideals and possibilities. In Christ's resurrection the Christian has also risen "in newness of life".

When we consider the contrast in Rom. 7.6 between the spirit and the letter, it is a little surprising to find Paul saying in 7.14: "We know that the law is spiritual." Law and spirit, we are apt to think, are mutually exclusive terms. The Christian lives in the Spirit, *therefore* he is not under the law. But Paul never forgets that in certain relations and for certain purposes, the law is divine. That is what he means here when he says that it is πνευματικός. It is spiritual in its essence, though not in its form, so there can only be a spiritual fulfilment of it. The unredeemed man, who is σαρκικός—a creature of flesh sold under sin—can make nothing of it. If his religion, or philosophical outlook, is determined by the law, then his nature stands in no proper relation to his ideals; the position is one in which he is doomed to endless defeat and ultimate despair. The law which is "spiritual" in essence has its spiritual power neutralized by the form in which it addresses itself to man. The law may be in itself spiritual, but it does not come to him with the power which

1 Rom. 14.17.
2 Rom. 12.12; cf. 5.2.

properly belongs to spirit. The Holy Spirit, according to Paul, is essentially life-giving, but, as he says elsewhere, the law is unable to give life.[1] Had there been such a thing, had there been a law which possessed the power to fulfil its own requirements—in other words, had there been a law which was "spiritual" in the full sense of the term—righteousness would no doubt have come by it; man would not have been left to fulfil his vocation alone; as it arose before his mind the power of God would have risen simultaneously in his heart to realize it. But with all his recognition of the fact that the law came from God and expressed his will, Paul had no experience of this kind when he lived under the law; life under the law, spiritual as he acknowledged the law to be, and for a time delighting in it "after the inner man", had become for him a life of frustration, ending in despair. All his experiences of the Spirit as the divine power through which the law of God is accomplished dated from his acquaintance with Christ.

This is the point to which we are brought at the beginning of chapter 8. The Spirit is described in 8.2 as "the Spirit of life", or perhaps as "the Spirit of the life in Christ Jesus". In respect of meaning there is no appreciable difference. If we speak of the Spirit of life because he is essentially life and through the activity of the Holy Spirit there comes a divine power, then whether the phrase should be connected with Christ or not we can only hold that it is the same life in which Jesus triumphed over sin and death. The gift of the Spirit involves our participation in that triumph. "The law of the Spirit of life in Christ Jesus sets us free from the law of sin and death."

Karl Barth has drawn attention in his book *The Holy Spirit and the Christian Life* to a remarkable activity of the Holy Spirit in our lives. In Rom. 8 the Holy Spirit is described not merely as the inspiration of our prayers, but as an actual co-operator in prayer with us, so that we may justifiably say

[1] Gal. 3.21.

that it is not *I*, but *we* who pray—I and the Holy Spirit. The
distinction between the human spirit and the activity of the
Holy Spirit is emphasized by a reference to his function as a
witness to our divine sonship: "but ye received the spirit of
adoption, whereby we cry Abba Father. The Spirit himself
beareth witness with our spirit, that we are children of God:
and if children, then heirs; heirs of God, and joint heirs with
Christ."[1] Paul then passes on to describe, in graphic terms,
the agonizing character of unassisted human prayer: "we
ourselves groan within ourselves."[2] But the Holy Spirit comes
to our aid: "And in like manner the Spirit also helpeth our
infirmity: for we know not how to pray as we ought; but the
Spirit himself maketh intercession for us with groanings which
cannot be uttered."[3] This human prayer, reinforced by the
intercession of the Holy Spirit, is answered by God because
such prayer is in accordance with the divine will: "He
(God) that searcheth the hearts knoweth what is the mind of
the Spirit, because he (the Spirit) maketh intercession for the
saints according to the will of God."[4] The same thought
appears in the Epistle to the Ephesians: "praying at all seasons
in Spirit".[5] Parallel passages are found in Jude 20:
"but ye ... praying in the Holy Spirit"; and in Phil. 3.3:
"for we are the circumcision, who worship by the Spirit
of God".

Throughout Rom. 8 the regenerate spirit of man and the
indwelling Spirit of God are spoken of in one breath, as though
they were one and the same, yet the separate existence of the
Holy Spirit is clearly seen. Union with Christ is a fact founded
upon faith, or on baptism as the concrete act of faith;
but conscious union with Christ is the work of the Holy
Spirit. Conscious union with Christ involves the reality and

[1] Rom. 8.15–16.
[2] V. 23.
[3] V. 26.
[4] V. 27.
[5] Eph. 6.18.

consciousness of sonship on our part. The Holy Spirit in us cries, "Abba, Father".

THE SPIRIT AND THE LAW

We have seen that the Spirit is opposed to anything legal; no contrast is sharper in Paul's mind than that of spirit and letter. Yet the Spirit is not antinomian. There is a law of the Spirit even as there is a commandment of love. The Holy Spirit does indeed transcend everything statutory; in the originality of its activity all legal enactments are seen to be quite futile. But it legislates, nevertheless. The work of the Holy Spirit is seen in laying down the proper course of conduct for man. There is nothing mystical in the work of the Spirit, nothing which opens the door to antinomianism or moral anarchism. Indeed justice is done to the law by those who walk after the Spirit. It is in them that the righteous demand of the law is fulfilled. The law, which is spiritual, never gets justice done to it until man becomes the possessor of the Spirit, and then it gets justice done to it, not by any exertions of the man, nor by "works of the law", but by the impulse of the Spirit which brings his natural impotence to an end and enables him to live according to the mind of Christ (Rom. 8.4). The just demand of the law, as Paul puts it, is fulfilled in those who walk after the Spirit, *in* them, not *by* them. The realization that this change has been accomplished by God is shown not only by the reference to the Spirit, but also by the particular preposition used. It is the same attitude which finds expression in the words: "I live; and yet no longer I, but Christ liveth in me."[1]

It is not necessary here to discuss the grammatical details of the difficult and complicated sentence in 8.3.[2] The Revised Standard Version translates as follows: "For God has done what the law, weakened by the flesh, could not do: sending

[1] Gal. 1.20.
[2] See W. Sanday and A. C. Headlam, *Romans*, pp. 191 f.

his own Son in the likeness of sinful flesh and for sin, he condemned sin in the flesh." "Sinful flesh" describes man's nature as having become the seat of indwelling sin. But sin is no essential or necessary part of human nature, only its fault and corruption. That is why Christ could take human flesh at the time of the Incarnation: "The Word was made flesh." This "flesh" was without that quality of sinfulness which it has acquired in us, who are "naturally engendered of the offspring of Adam". Christ was thus sent in the *likeness* of sinful flesh, not as if he had taken on the semblance of body instead of its reality, but because the flesh of Christ, which committed no sin in itself, was like that which had sinned— like it in its nature, but not in the corruption which was "in Adam". There was therefore in Christ the same flesh as that whose nature in man is sinful.

There are two ways in which God condemned sin in the flesh: (i) By exhibiting in the person of his Incarnate Son the same flesh in reality but free from sin, he proved that sin "in the flesh" was unnatural and a usurping tyrant. Thus the manifestation of Christ in sinless humanity condemned sin in principle. But (ii) God condemned sin practically and effectually by destroying its power and casting it out: and this is the sense which is required in this context. The law could condemn sin only in word, and could not make its condemnation effectual. Christ coming "for sin" not only made atonement for it by his death, but uniting man to himself "in newness of life" gave actual effect to the condemnation of sin by destroying its dominion "in the flesh" through the life-giving sanctifying power of his Spirit.

THE SPIRIT AND THE FLESH

Throughout the eighth chapter the Spirit is contrasted sharply with the flesh. Those who are after the flesh mind the things of the flesh; those who are of the Spirit, the things of the Spirit. The mind of the flesh means death, the mind of the Spirit peace and life. We have already briefly discussed the "flesh" in connection with the law,[1] here we shall consider it in relation to the Holy Spirit with whom it is contrasted and in constant opposition.

The term "flesh" in a few passages undoubtedly refers to the bodily organism. Thus when Jesus is spoken of as being "of the seed of David according to the flesh"[2] it is physical descent or bodily form that is meant. The reference as regards circumcision "in the flesh" is similarly limited in meaning.[3] But as a general rule, "flesh" in Pauline thought stands for the active principle of sin in human nature, or for the sphere in which it is entrenched. The notion of weakness which belongs to the "flesh", as the Old Testament conceived it, made "flesh" the easy prey of sin which uses this acquired territory as its headquarters, and from it wages war against the inner man, employing the very members of man's body to procure his undoing.[4] Hence whether Paul uses the simple term "flesh" or the fuller phrase "flesh of sin", indicating the "flesh" as allied with sin, what he means far transcends any physical reference and can only mean human nature as a whole viewed as in active opposition to God. The "flesh" is as nearly as possible identical with what we sometimes call man's lower nature. For sin established in the "flesh" controls the whole man, and so there can be such a thing as "the mind of the flesh",[5] that is, thoughts which are under the influence of the baser self.

Now "flesh" with this ethical interpretation has its true antithesis in "spirit". The word πνεῦμα or spirit takes over the meaning of the Hebrew word *Ruah* which, in distinction

[1] See pp. 54 ff above.
[2] Rom. 1.3.
[3] Rom. 2.28.
[4] Rom. 7.23.
[5] Col. 2.18.

from *Nephesh*, expressed a man's personality on its more energetic side, especially that on which it was open to the action of the Spirit of God. As the work of the Holy Spirit took on more and more an ethical quality, there was a corresponding deepening in the conception of the human "spirit", with the result that the term came to mean for Paul man's moral and spiritual nature. It is sometimes difficult to know whether Paul is referring to the human spirit or the Spirit of God. In his view there is a "spirit" which is so much man's property that he can speak of "my", "thy", or "your" spirit.[1] Christians can be assured that "the Spirit himself bears witness with our spirit, that we are the children of God".[2] Such a human spirit, however, represents at best a possibility rather than a power. In itself it is incapable of achieving the mastery, for the "flesh", made stronger by the demands of the law, tyrannizes over the spirit and keeps it in bondage.

The only hope of mastery over the flesh is to be found in the work of the Holy Spirit. What the law could not do, in that it was weak when opposed by the "flesh", Christ has done, in that by his death he has passed sentence on the sin which has entrenched itself in man.[3] That condemnation becomes a realized experience to all who by faith unite themselves with Christ, for not only are they "planted" with him in his death, but they also share in the victory of his resurrection. It is the Holy Spirit which raised Christ from the dead which is given to them in baptism and dwells in them, so toning up and energizing their "spirit" that it becomes the regnant element in their nature and life. It is through the indwelling of the Holy Spirit that they are no longer "in the flesh but in the Spirit";[4] they are "spiritual" men in whom the "spirit" has come to its rightful place and power.

[1] 1 Cor. 5.4; 2 Cor. 7.13; Philemon 25; 1 Thess. 5.23.
[2] Rom. 8.16.
[3] Rom. 8.3.
[4] Rom. 8.9.

ESCHATOLOGY AND THE SPIRIT

Now it is clear that to some extent Paul idealizes the situation. We have argued that when Paul speaks of a man being "dead unto sin" he is speaking the truth sacramentally and eschatologically.[1] It is the Holy Spirit who is the pledge of sanctification in Christ in the Kingdom of Heaven. Rom. 8.15–17 shows how easily the Apostle's mind moved from the subject of the Spirit and the Spirit's indwelling to that of the glorified existence which is the Christian's goal. He says: "Ye received the spirit of adoption, whereby we cry, Abba, Father. The Spirit himself beareth witness with our spirit, that we are the children of God: and if children, then heirs: heirs of God, and joint heirs with Christ; if so be that we suffer with him, that we may be also glorified with him." He defines the Spirit which has been bestowed upon them as that which makes them realize that already they are the sons of God. But what does the status of being sons of God mean for those who have been baptized?[2] The ultimate meaning is clearly expressed in the final clause of the verse, "glorified with him". We have a parallel with this in 1 John 3.2: "Beloved now are we children of God, and it is not yet manifest what we shall be. We know that, if he shall be manifested, we shall be like him." The last clause corresponds exactly with that which we have emphasized in the verse above. The future "glory" of the sons of God is really synonymous with "likeness to Christ". But this likeness to Christ is the content of the "spiritual body" for Paul. It is the σῶμα σαρκικόν which prevents the sons of God from reaching their true end. For that reason the Apostle in Phil. 3.21 speaks of himself as "eagerly awaiting the Lord Jesus Christ who shall fashion

---

[1] See pp. 112 ff above.

[2] Although there is no specific mention of baptism in this passage it is to be noted that W. Sanday and A. C. Headlam, *Romans*, p. 201, paraphrase verse 14 as follows: "When you were first baptised, and the communication of the Holy Spirit sealed your admission into the Christian fold . . . ."

anew the body of our humiliation, that it may be conformed
to the body of his glory". As soon as the σῶμα σαρκικόν has
been exchanged for the spiritual body, which is equivalent to
the body of his glory, the Christian shall have entered into his
inheritance.

This conception also finds expression in Rom. 8.23: "We
ourselves also, which have the firstfruits of the Spirit, even we
ourselves groan within ourselves, waiting for our adoption, to
wit, the redemption of our body." Christians in virtue of their
baptismal justification have the firstfruits consisting in the
Spirit. This is very similar to 2 Cor. 1.22 where Paul, emphasizing the faithfulness of God, speaks of him as giving us
"the pledge" of the Spirit in our hearts. What is the "firstfruits" of which Paul speaks in the Epistle to the Romans?
Obviously the "sonship" which is expressly defined as the
redemption of the body. The possession of the Spirit, which is
the pledge or firstfruits of the sonship, points beyond the
present to the complete realization of sonship which means
the redemption of the body. The sonship is therefore an all-
embracing conception; it affects not only the spirit but the
body. It applies to the whole person in Paul's judgement. The
body is to be Christ's as well as the spirit. The body is to
share in the divine nature, not however as a σῶμα σαρκικόν
but as a σῶμα πνευματικόν. It has to be redeemed as well
as the soul.

In this, as always, Christ is the forerunner of his disciples.
He has entered upon his full inheritance; he has vindicated
his position of Sonship. And in Rom. 1.4, Paul gives a description of this process: "Declared to be the Son of God with
power, according to the spirit of holiness, by the resurrection
of the dead." The resurrection of Jesus Christ is here designated by the striking phrase, "the resurrection of the dead",
implying that he is only the first of a series, the type of what
should follow. It is this which marks him out as the Son of
God. The resurrection was the inevitable consequence of his

possession of the Spirit of holiness, which he possessed without measure. As risen he appeared to his disciples in the body of glory, the body which was the outward expression of the Spirit of holiness. It was natural that the Apostle should make that experience the basis of his thought concerning the future life of believers. If they are to be "joint-heirs with Christ", they must share in Christ's exaltation. In view of the fact that the "flesh" of Jesus was never stained with sin, the glorifying of his body might have been taken for granted, what is so wonderful, and this is part of the good news Paul had to proclaim, is that the Christian, whose body of flesh seemed to be the very seed-plot of all sinful desires and passions, should also share in that glory, the redemption of the body. To have a sure pledge that the body would one day be redeemed was indeed a matter for rejoicing.

There is a passage in Paul's Epistle to the Ephesians which is worth considering in this connection. In Eph. 1.14, he writes: "In whom [i.e. Christ] ye were sealed with the Holy Spirit of promise, which is an earnest of your inheritance, unto the redemption of God's possession,[1] unto the praise of his glory." The Holy Spirit, who is here regarded as having been bestowed upon the Christian in baptism,[2] is designated as the Spirit of promise, an earnest[3] of our inheritance. The inheritance can be nothing else, in view of what we have said, than the sonship in which believers are to follow the Captain of their salvation. The function of the Spirit is to point forward, to make the Christian sure of the fulfilment of what he already possesses.

---

[1] Περιποίησις is usually interpreted as being God's People. But it is possible to correlate περιποιήσεως with σώματος in Rom. 8.23. The context never goes beyond the personal reference ἡμεῖς or ὑμεῖς.

[2] The word σφραγίζομαι is generally understood to refer to baptism, see E. F. Scott, *Colossians, Philemon and Ephesians* (1930), pp. 148, 223 f.

[3] The word translated "earnest" (ἀρραβών) means "a part given in advance of what will be bestowed fully afterwards", J. H. Moulton and G. Milligan, *Vocabulary of the Greek Testament* (1930).

It is clear then that the work of the Holy Spirit when brought into association with baptism should be placed in an eschatological setting. The writers of the New Testament thought that the "New Age" had broken in upon this world with the coming of Christ. The forces of evil had been defeated by the Son of God upon the Cross. That was indeed "good news", but the early Church went a step further by asserting that the blessings of this "New Age" were shared by all who surrendered themselves to Christ in faith. This fact, as we have seen, is expressed and achieved in the sacrament of baptism. That which was formerly regarded as being reserved for God's people in some distant future, was now seen to be available for every believer in this present life.

The popular phrase "realized eschatology"[1] was coined to describe this change in religious outlook which had been brought about by the teaching, life, death, and resurrection of Jesus Christ. There is, however, a danger lest the emphasis on the word "realized" should be so heavy that it suppresses the original meaning of the word "eschatology". In the gospels there is still present the idea of an ultimate fulfilment of the Kingdom of Heaven at the consummation of the present age. This is true of the Fourth Evangelist who more than the other evangelists stresses the fact that eternal life or the Kingdom of Heaven is present here and now. "He that believeth *hath* eternal life."[2] The present quality of salvation is emphasized, but he does not lose sight of the doctrine of the Second Advent.[3] It is evident that the hope expressed by the early Church in its belief that Jesus would return in power and glory, is not regarded by the Fourth Evangelist as being fully

---

[1] R. H. Fuller in *The Mission and Achievement of Jesus*, pp. 79 ff, rejects the phrase "realized eschatology". W. G. Kümmel, *Promise and Fulfilment* (1957), p. 109, argues that our Lord teaches that the Kingdom of God is already a present reality in his own person.

[2] John 6.47.

[3] John 5.27-9; 17.24.

10

satisfied in the present experience of Christ through the coming of the Spirit.[1]

It would perhaps be best to use the phrase "proleptic eschatology"[2] as suggesting the fact that the blessings of the "New Age" are anticipated in the life of the believer, but await fulfilment when Christ shall come again in glory. This is what is implied in the passages on the work of the Holy Spirit which we have examined. The newness of life which is given by the Spirit at the moment of baptismal justification is the first instalment of what will be enjoyed more fully in the future. It may still seem strange that we can speak of the fullness of salvation being enjoyed by the believer at the moment of baptism and yet go on to say that the full fruits of Christ's saving work still lie in the future. But this is in complete accord with the New Testament conception of holiness.[3]

THE MEANING OF HOLINESS

In the epistles of Paul and the Book of Revelation, in the Acts and the Epistle to the Hebrews, Church members generally are called saints or holy persons. This is very conspicuous in 1 Cor. 1.2, "to the church of God, men sanctified in Christ Jesus, which is at Corinth, called to be saints". Yet in 3.1, the Corinthians are described as men of flesh, as babes in Christ, and therefore incapable of the spiritual food fit only for the perfect, i.e. men in Christ.

The significance of the word "holy" as a description of the Christian life, and a solution to this apparent contradiction, are to be found in the holy objects of the Old Covenant, e.g. the Sabbath, the tabernacle, the sacrifices, and the priesthood. All these were devoted unreservedly to the service of God.

---

[1] Cf. John 14.16 ff.
[2] H. V. Martin, *Expository Times*, li, pp. 88 ff.
[3] See my article in *Theology*, xxv, 205, pp. 13 ff.

They are thus symbols of the unreserved devotion which Christ demands of his followers. These last are a priesthood offering their bodies as a living sacrifice. So 1 Pet. 2.5, "A holy priesthood, to offer up spiritual sacrifices", and Rom. 12.1, "present your bodies a living sacrifice, holy, acceptable to God, your rational service". In other words, the holiness set before the servants of God is unreserved devotion to God and his work.

On the other hand, whatever men might do, the holy objects which are claimed for God's service were placed in a new and solemn relation to himself. Men might desecrate the Sabbath, or the Sanctuary, or the Priesthood, but they were holy still, and their indelible sanctity condemned those who defiled them. In this very real sense *objective* holiness belongs to all baptized members of Christ's Church. They have acquired an indelible character in virtue of their baptismal justification. In this most common sense of the word they are spoken of as "saints" or "holy persons". Occasionally, however, we find holiness set before men as a goal to be pursued and attained. The word then denotes actual unreserved loyalty to Christ. This is the *subjective* holiness to which Christ calls his servants.

Furthermore, even in regard to this subjective holiness, perfection in the New Testament is never spoken of in an absolute sense, it is a relative term and depends on the man himself and the circumstances in which he is placed. In one case it is indiscriminate beneficence,[1] like the beneficence of the God of nature. In another it is the surrender of all material goods.[2] Elsewhere it is the endurance or trial of faith;[3] and in another place the perfect man is one who has complete control of his tongue,[4] while the perfection which fits a man to

[1] Matt. 5.45–8.
[2] Mark 10.23–6.
[3] Jas. 1.4.
[4] Jas. 3.2.

apprehend wisdom will lift him above the petty contentions such as divided the Church at Corinth.[1] It must therefore be moral in content as well as intellectual. The maturity which the Apostle desired of the Ephesians would have saved them from vacillation and error in doctrine.[2]

Different though these descriptions of the Christian character may be, they are closely related, as each has its object in union with God in Christ. There is set before men a moral and spiritual ideal suited to everyone in every position in life and according to every age. Each upward step reveals heights higher still; as each step is made, as maturity is gained in one stage of spiritual growth, new grace is given for further and more rapid pursuit of the goal that lies ahead. Paul, while asserting that he no longer lives, but that Christ lives in him, still presses forward to a loftier goal. In this he presents himself a pattern for full grown men in Christ. Each τέλος both in revelation and in experience is also an ἀρχή, a beginning. There is nothing legalistic or static about the Christian life. The perfection of the believer can never be identical with absolute perfection; that belongs to God alone. Perfection for the Christian is maturity, being complete in all parts and powers according to the stage that has been reached.

Thus we can see how the new life which began at baptism with an act of full and complete surrender to Christ can be called holy and perfect and yet at the same time develop as the Christian soul grows in maturity. There will always be room for growth, even after this life has ended, for the grace of God is inexhaustible and the riches of Christ unsearchable.

Such eschatological thoughts lead us on, as it led Paul on, to a consideration of the working out of God's purpose in history especially with reference to the fulfilment of his promises towards the people of Israel. It is this that we shall consider in the next chapter.

[1] 1 Cor. 2.6.
[2] Eph. 4.12.

8

THE RIGHTEOUSNESS OF GOD
IN HISTORY

THE PURPOSE OF GOD AND HIS NATURE

THE foundation of Paul's life was his belief in God as the ultimate cause and final purpose of all things. The Christian salvation, which brings forgiveness, holiness, freedom, and blessedness to men, and which comes through the person and work, the crucifixion and resurrection of Jesus Christ, is rooted in, and springs out of the absolute and perfect will of God. Paul knew that his life in Christ had its source in the very being of God. Hence his tone of certainty and courage. "We *know* that to them that love God all things work together for good, even to them that are called according to his purpose. For whom he foreknew, he also foreordained to be conformed to the Image of his Son, that he might be the firstborn among many brethren: and whom he foreordained, them also he called: and whom he called, them also he justified: and whom he justified, them also he glorified."[1] It was in the interests of his own certainty of salvation in Christ that he developed his conception of the purpose of God, for the purpose of God expresses his nature. How then did Paul conceive God?

It was not necessary for him to formulate any doctrine of God; for he could take for granted the conception of God

---

[1] Rom. 8.28–30.

which he believed to have been given in the Old Testament.
He assumed also the revelation of God given in Christ. God
is Father and it is in Christ that men receive this revelation
of God. A question which is sometimes asked nowadays would
probably have been meaningless to him. If he had been asked,
Is God's Fatherhood universal or not? he would doubtless
have answered, It is only in Christ that God has made himself
known to me as Father, and it is only in Christ that I can live
the life of a child of God. This is the only answer which the
Christian can give. The Father is love and that love has been
shown in and through the sacrifice of Christ upon the Cross.
"God commendeth his own love towards us, in that, while we
were yet sinners, Christ died for us."[1] From that love no
power can separate the believer. "I am persuaded, that
neither death, nor life, nor angels, nor principalities, nor things
present, nor things to come, nor powers, nor height, nor
depth, nor any other creature, shall be able to separate us
from the love of God, which is in Christ Jesus our Lord."[2]
The scope of that love is universal: "God hath shut up all
unto disobedience, that he might have mercy on all."[3] This
merciful love of God becomes personally effective in each man
in God's grace. "Being justified freely by his grace through
the redemption that is in Christ Jesus."[4]

If we ask why the grace of God must express itself in Christ's
sacrifice upon the Cross, the answer lies in Paul's conception
of the divine righteousness as including both wrath and love.
Paul knew that God in his forbearance had passed over men's
sins done in the past.[5] It is through the sacrifice of Christ
that he reveals what had always been his attitude to sin as
well as his love for men. Mercy and wrath;[6] grace and judge-

[1] Rom. 5.8.
[2] Rom. 8.38,39.
[3] Rom. 11.32.
[4] Rom. 3.24.
[5] Rom. 3.25; cf. Acts 17.30.
[6] Rom. 1.18.

ment were expressed by God in the single act of the death of Christ. The love of God is holy because the divine reaction against sin is judgement upon the sinner; but it is love because in the person of Christ he endures the wrath and the judgement himself that he may forgive and save. The whole purpose of God in human history is consummated in this revelation of the righteousness of God.

But how is this revelation related to God's revelation of himself in the Old Testament? This has already been considered, here we would further add that Paul asserts the continuity of God's purpose in two ways. First, he teaches that the gospel was the fulfilment of the promise made to Abraham, which was antecedent to, and so could not be superseded by, the law.[1] The recipient of this promise, Abraham, was saved by faith in the same way as those who by faith accept its fulfilment in Christ. "Abraham believed God, and it was reckoned unto him for righteousness."[2] Secondly, the law which "came in beside" discharged a necessary historical function in relation to the fulfilment of the promise. In provoking and condemning sin it made man more fully aware of his need for the grace of God, and so the law was a preparation for the gospel. This argument translated into modern terms means that moral discipline is necessary to enable men to grow in their filial relationship to God, and it is this relationship which is the ultimate purpose of God's dealings with men, while the preparatory discipline is but a means.

GOD'S PURPOSE UNIVERSAL

There is, however, a difference: the law was apparently the exclusive possession of God's Chosen People whereas the

[1] Gal. 3.17.
[2] Rom. 4.3.

gospel is offered to all mankind. How is this extension of God's purpose to be explained? Paul answers in two ways: First, he asks, "Is this blessing then pronounced upon the circumcision, or upon the uncircumcision also? for we say, To Abraham his faith was reckoned for righteousness. How then was it reckoned? when he was in circumcision or in uncircumcision? Not in circumcision, but in uncircumcision: and he received the sign of circumcision, a seal of the righteousness of faith which he had while he was in uncircumcision: that he might be the father of all them that believe, though they be in uncircumcision, that righteousness might be reckoned unto them: and the father of uncircumcision to them who not only are of the circumcision, but also walk in the steps of that faith of our father Abraham which he had in uncircumcision."[1] This means that the moral and spiritual disposition which welcomes the gospel and receives the grace of God offered in Jesus Christ is not dependent upon any national privilege or racial peculiarity. All men are capable of faith, and so the gospel can be offered to all men for their acceptance. The Rabbinical form of Paul's argument should not hide its essential soundness; it was as man, not as Jew that Abraham believed. In the second place, Paul so universalized the idea of the law that he could use it in his appeal to the Gentiles. The Law of God in a certain sense was known by the pagan world. In the first chapter of Romans he describes God's revelation of himself in terms of natural law, and in the second chapter in terms of conscience. He maintains that such revelation was full enough to leave no excuse for the idolatry and corruption of the Gentiles, and adequate to produce the conviction of sin in the hearts of those who had never heard of the Mosaic Law. The modern missionary enterprise has proved that there is no race of men whose innate characteristics prevent them from responding to the gospel. To this extent Paul's argument is a valid one, though we may

[1] Rom. 4.9–12.

doubt his contention that the revelation has been so full and definite as to make man's ignorance of God inexcusable.

THE PROBLEM OF JEWISH UNBELIEF

This universal nature of the gospel at once poses two important questions to Paul's critical mind. As he looked out upon the wide sweep of his vision, upon the eternal purpose of God to make all men partakers of the promise in Jesus Christ, he was faced with the actual rejection of Christ by official Judaism. The unbelief of Israel, taken along with the extensive acceptance of the gospel by the Gentiles suggested that Israel's election had been cancelled and that God had not been faithful to his promise. Or, if it did not suggest this, was there not an argument against his gospel to this effect: the gospel which Paul was preaching cannot in fact be true, for it was rejected by the mass of the Chosen People.

Paul was too honest to shirk the problem and he deals with it in chapters 9, 10, and 11. In these chapters he is popularly supposed to be justifying the ways of God to men, by asserting his absolute rights, as against any power on man's part to control his destiny. "It is not of him that willeth, nor of him that runneth, but of God that showeth mercy." "Hath not the potter power over the clay?" Such a conception of God's absolute sovereignty annihilates human freedom and re-sponsibility, and thus, in fact, Paul has constantly been regarded, by those within and without the Church, as really denying the bases of moral action. This has resulted in a misuse of Paul by those who are prepared to be "Calvinistic" and an equally serious misuse of his teaching by those who are not. But in fact this popular interpretation of Paul's meaning is an error due to a failure to keep a clear idea of the (ideal) opponent's position in view. The opponent whom Paul has in mind is a Jew, or one representing the Jewish case, who pleads that God had pledged himself to the Jews as such: he had committed himself to them as the Chosen People; it was enough for them to say, "We have Abraham for our father"; "the temple of the Lord are we". Thus, any view of God's dealings which involved the conclusion that the Church of the New Testament and not the Jewish race constituted under present circumstances the elect body, on a basis of faith and not of the law, stood self-condemned. Now such a plea as the Jew is here supposed to have urged, carries with it the supposition that God had tied his hands in choosing Israel. However Israel might behave, God was committed to it. As against such a position—a position really destructive of all moral responsibility—Paul asserts the divine freedom. He asserts that God never tied his hands by committing himself to the material limits of a race, in such a way as that men could rest indolently on the covenant. Thus the main point of Paul's argument is to emphasize the sense of responsibility by making it plain that God's election is a challenge to faith and not a substitute for it.

THE ELECTION OF ISRAEL NOT CANCELLED

In the first place, the argument is directed to the hypothesis of God cancelling the election of Israel. Paul guards against this inference from the facts by three distinct arguments. The first of these is that there was always an election within the election; the second, that in election God is sovereign and not under law to the elect; the third, that if Israel was rejected it was her own fault; she had brought it upon herself by acts of disobedience and unbelief for which she had a bad reputation all through her history.

There always was an election within the election. This is the gist of 9.6–9. What the Apostle says here is in substance as follows: It is certainly a serious thing to speak of Israel's election as being cancelled, for that would seem to imply that God's word declaring Israel to be his peculiar people had been made void. But we must distinguish between election after the flesh and election which is of promise. There is an election which can rightly be cancelled, and an election which cannot be cancelled, an outer circle which may be effaced, and an inner circle that is ineffaceable. There always have been these two elections, the outer and the inner, an Israel of God within the Israel after the flesh, a seed of Jacob the child of promise within the seed of Abraham. Ishmael was rejected, Isaac chosen: Esau was rejected and Jacob chosen, antecedently to all moral conduct, though both were of the same mother and father. These two elements can be traced throughout the course of Israel's history; they can be seen at the present time. There is an Israel after the flesh, and an Israel after the promise at the very time Paul is writing. And it is of the former only that the cancelling of the election can be asserted. The election within the election stands, for this inner circle is to be found within the catholic Church, consisting of both Jews and Gentiles, the middle wall of partition between them having been broken down through Jesus Christ.[1] It cannot therefore be said now that the word of God calling Israel to be the chosen race has been rendered void, except in the sense that the same thing could have been said at any time in Israel's history, for example, in the time of Elijah.

Paul's imaginary opponent may well at this point have asked, But isn't such arbitrary selectiveness unfair? Paul answers this in 9.10–24, the leading thought of which is that in the act of electing God is free; that as no people has a claim to be elected, so no people has a claim to the continuance of the election; that what God sovereignly begins he may sovereignly end. There may be good reasons why God should not end what he has solemnly begun, but they are to be found in God and not in man. Man cannot create or dictate his own vocation. Viewed externally, one class or nation may have a higher and wider sphere of opportunity than another.

[1] Cf. Eph. 2.14.

Viewed internally, as a matter of individual relation to God, there is no respect of persons. Each man is dealt with equally in view of his opportunities. There are those who are first in privilege who shall be last in acceptance, and last in privilege who shall be first in acceptance. But viewed externally, as a matter of external privilege, one class is dealt with differently from another. And the selection of men for the various degrees of privilege, for the various parts they play in the drama of the world, lies absolutely in the inscrutable choice of God.

Paul, in his endeavour to beat down Jewish pride, asserts this sovereignty of God in an absolute and peremptory manner. Going back to the commencement of Israel's history, he shows how plainly God's sovereignty is asserted even there, inasmuch as it determined which of the two sons about to be borne by Rebecca was to be the heir of the promise before the children were born, therefore before anything in the conduct of the two sons had emerged to make the election turn on personal merit. The elder, it was announced beforehand, was to serve the younger, so excluding not merely personal character but civil law and custom as the ground of choice.[1] This appears at first sight arbitrary and even unrighteous, but the Apostle at this moment is not concerned about that. In his keenness to answer his imaginary opponent, he merely points out what is found in the actual history of the Jews. He even goes on to show that it was not a solitary instance of sovereign action, pointing out that God claimed the right of so acting in all cases by quoting the words, "I will have mercy on whom I will have mercy."[2] He then cites the case of Pharaoh

[1] "The absolute election of Jacob has reference simply to the election of one to higher privileges as head of the chosen race, than the other. It has nothing to do with their eternal salvation. In the original to which Paul is referring Esau is simply a synonym for Edom." See W. Sanday and A. C. Headlam, *Romans*, p. 245. Cf. G. Schrenk, *Theologisches Wörterbuch zum Neuen Testament* iv, p. 184: "It is not here a question of their becoming saved, but of their historical position and task in life."

[2] Rom. 9.15.

in proof that God acts on that principle not merely to the positive effect of sovereignly exercising mercy, but also in the negative effect of hardening men's hearts to destruction. To the Christian this is a perplexing statement and prompts the objection: if this is so, what personal responsibility can anyone have for sin? Once again we must remember the imaginary opponent. No doubt if Paul had been thinking of a genuine inquirer who was concerned about the equilibrium between divine sovereignty and human responsibility, he would have modified and adjusted his statement. Had he been in the mood to pursue this line of thought with a view to reconciling divine sovereignty with divine love on the one hand, and with human responsibility on the other hand, he could easily have found materials for the purpose even in God's dealings with the king of Egypt. The purpose of the signs and wonders performed by Moses was to soften Pharaoh's heart to let the Children of Israel go. Pharaoh's heart was hardened by means fitted and intended to have the opposite effect. That this should have happened is no isolated case. What is intended to soften men's hearts often has the opposite effect. Paul was aware of this as well as we are, but he was not in the mood to make conciliatory statements, or to qualify the absoluteness of his remarks. He was dealing with a proud man who thought that the election of the people of Israel gave him and his fellow Jews a pre-scriptive right to divine favour. So instead of softening what he has said he goes on to make a harder statement still; he rep-resents God as a potter, and men as clay, out of which God can make such vessels as he pleases—one for a higher use, another for a lower. Who shall complain if vessels which, whatever high uses they were destined for, are in fact found only fit to be thrown away, are at last, after fullest trial, unable to be used, and others taken in their place which, though up to now kept in the background, had been made for glorious ends. The prophets had constantly warned the Jews that God's choice would fall upon those who were "not his people", and that the true Israel was to be found in "the remnant".

Even so, we must notice carefully the exact expressions used in this passage. The perfect κατηρτισμένα (9.22) means that a certain state has been reached, not necessarily that a certain purpose has been accomplished. Though the vessels are "ready" for destruction, Paul does not say either that God was responsible for their condition or that they were destroyed. Paul was aware that human souls are not the same as lifeless clay. In Eph. 2.3 he asserts that those who now accept the Christian faith were formerly "by nature children of wrath". In other words, "vessels of wrath" may become "vessels of mercy". The apparent hardness of the saying is justified as Paul was attacking human arrogance, but as an exact and complete statement of the relations between God and man it cannot, of course, be so regarded.[1]

How far the Apostle was from intending to teach fatalism appears from his third argument, the purpose of which is to throw the blame of Israel's rejection on herself. This argument forms the main content of chapter 10. He here brings against Israel the charge of rebelling voluntarily against the righteousness of God. Paul fully recognizes the contribution which his people have made in preparing for the coming of Christ in their zeal and enthusiasm for the righteousness of the law. He nevertheless holds his countrymen responsible for the great miscarriage of their vocation, finding in their passion for righteousness not only a lack of knowledge or spiritual insight, for which they might have been excused, but a culpable spirit of self-will. He ascribes to them the ambition to establish a righteousness which they can regard as their own achievement. They were too proud to acknowledge their dependence upon God. They were, in fact, unbelievers, not because they had

---

[1] C. K. Barrett, *Romans*, p. 188, calls this a detail in the analogy, the major comparison being "between the final responsibility of the potter for what he produces, and the final responsibility of God for what he does in history".

not heard the gospel or had not understood its meaning. They had heard and had understood only too well. The present unbelief is but a reproduction of a characteristic feature of the Jewish people in every generation. Moses had warned them, "I will provoke you to jealousy with that which is no nation, with a nation void of understanding will I provoke you",[1] thus hinting a threat of degradation from the position of being the elect race. Isaiah still more challengingly had spoken of a divine purpose of disinheritance by pointing on the one hand to the honour God had received from foreigners, and, on the other hand, to the indifference and even hostility with which his messages had been received by the chosen nation.[2] These quotations show that unbelief and disobedience had been characteristic features of the people of Israel all through their history, provoking God to regret his choice and to threaten their disinheritance. These same characteristics re-appear in the present generation in an exaggerated form for they have rejected the looked-for Messiah himself in the person of Jesus Christ. So far God had been very patient but now his patience is all but exhausted, "all day long did I spread out my hands unto a disobedient and gainsaying people."[3]

THE RESTORATION OF ISRAEL

Paul had been on the point of saying that God had indeed cast off his people.[4] But at this point the argument takes a new turn. He recoils from the idea of an absolute and final act of disinheritance, he finds even in the prophetic sayings a gleam of hope upon which to build a brighter future. Looked at broadly the prophetic utterances had seemed to suggest complete rejection; but was that what the prophets had actually said? Looking at the matter again Paul comes to the conclusion that God does not cast away his people.

[1] Rom. 10.19.   [2] Rom. 10.20,21.   [3] Rom. 10.21.
[4] Rom. 11.1.

"I say then, did God cast off his people? God forbid." He speaks vehemently, and he has a good right. He himself is an Israelite, of the seed of Abraham, of the tribe of Benjamin. He had not been cast away, but accepted by God. For he remembers his own history, that of one who had also been unbelieving and disobedient, and he cannot hope but that God who had mercy upon him, has grace in store also for his fellow countrymen, in spite of their provocations; he himself had been one who had persecuted Jesus in the person of the Church. Moved at once by patriotism, and by the hope inspired by his own conversion, he sets himself to put as encouraging a construction upon the facts as possible.

In the first place, he lays stress on the mere fact of election. "God did not cast off his people which he foreknew."[1] He has already combated the idea that the act of election gives the elected a claim to perpetual enjoyment of the privilege. But he also believes that an act of election may bring God under obligation to himself, though, as he points out later, not in a mechanical and impersonal way. Nevertheless, it is a strong point in favour of any people that God had foreknown or chosen it to a unique position among the nations of the world. From this point of view it can be said that "the gifts and calling of God are without repentance".[2] But in what way? This question leads on to Paul's second point. He extracts an answer from a consideration of the history of the Chosen People in Elijah's time. When Elijah thought that he stood alone in a faithless and apostate time, there were seven thousand men who had not bowed the knee to Baal—a small number, perhaps, as compared with the whole nation, but a great number compared with one man. "Even so then at this present time also there is a Remnant according to the election of grace."[3] In Elijah's day the Remnant consisted of those who voluntarily remained faithful to Yahweh. The true Israel, therefore, consists not automatically of those who belong to the

[1] Rom. 11.1.   [2] Rom. 11.29.   [3] Rom. 11.5.

Jewish nation, but those who are loyal to Yahweh's word. The same principle holds good to-day. In fact it goes back to our Lord's own teaching. In Mark 4.11 ff the mystery of election is expressed in these words: "Unto you is given the mystery of the kingdom of God: but unto them that are without, all things are done in parables: that seeing they may see and not perceive; and hearing they may hear and not understand; lest haply they should turn again and it should be forgiven them." This is so close to the teaching of Rom. 9—11 that many commentators feel that it has been influenced by Paul. Taylor doubts this on the ground that Mark does not speak of the hardening of Israel and Paul does not allude to the use of parables.[1] The strong Palestinian flavour of the Markan saying suggests that even if it is not an authentic saying of our Lord it at least gives a summary of his teaching on this matter. The doctrine of the Remnant finds its climax in the Person of Christ who when he hung upon the Cross was Israel, the Chosen People. He alone was faithful. But from the moment that those who by faith were incorporated into him they became members of the Chosen People and God's promises were fulfilled in them. So Paul thinks now of the Remnant, and this is his answer to those who maintained that the calling of God was "without repentance". He finds the calling to depend not on the unconditional acceptance of the race of Abraham, but on the basis of moral responsibility and its fulfilment in the Church.

It may seem surprising that Paul does not use the word ἐκκλησία in this epistle, except in Rom.16 where it is used of the local Church. Yet the idea of the Church "inspires his thought on every page".[2] It is the key to the understanding of

[1] V. Taylor, *The Gospel according to St Mark* (1953), p. 257.

[2] F. J. Leenhardt, *The Epistle to the Romans* (E.T. 1961), p. 21. It is to be observed that the Fourth Evangelist likewise does not use the word ἐκκλησία. Yet no one could have laid more emphasis than does John upon the conceptions which were most fundamental to the Christian idea of the Church. See my *The Religious Thought of St John*, pp. 160 ff.

Paul's conception of the purpose of God. That purpose was to bring into being a People whose relation to him would be one of faith, obedience, and love. In Abraham, "the father of the faithful", the Church had been both promised and in principle realized. Although theologians nowadays often speak of the New Israel as though the Church of the New Testament was discontinuous with the Church of the Old Testament, the phrase is never used in the New Testament. "There can be a new covenant with Israel, a new commandment given, a new Jerusalem, and even a new creation, but not a new Israel."[1] This emphasizes the continuity of the purpose of God in the two Testaments and subsequent history of the Church. The Church as the true Israel is the place where, in the mind of Paul, Jews and Gentiles are to be united in one body. It is universal in character and destined to include all mankind.

Even so the fact remained that in Paul's day the great majority of the Jewish nation were unbelievers. Paul is very concerned about this and in what follows we catch a glimpse of his love for the souls of men. He is not content with the salvation of the Remnant; he is deeply concerned about the rest of his countrymen.

He sorrowfully acknowledged that they have been blinded by inveterate prejudice, in accordance with the witness of Holy Scripture.[2] The picture of a blind, decrepit old man, bowed down with age and infirmity, suggested by the concluding words of the quotation from Ps. 69, is a very pathetic representation of a people in a state of religious senility. When a people gets to this senile condition in religion, its inevitable fate, one would say, is to stumble and fall; for blind old age cannot see the obstacles in the way, nor recover its balance when it stumbles.

Is Israel's doom, then, to stumble and fall and die, like an

---

[1] C. F. Evans, "Christology and Theology", in *The Communication of the Gospel in New Testament Times* (1961), p. 18.

[2] Rom. 11.7–10.

old man when his powers begin to fail? That is the question
the Apostle has to face. This he will not believe and he repels
the idea with another, "God forbid". But is it that he simply
will not believe it in spite of all the facts being loaded against
him? Or has he some shadow of reason to support him? The
prospect of finding such a reason seems small, and Paul is
obviously conscious that he has a difficult task in front of him.
His "I say then's" and his "God forbids" are the sure sign of
heavy going.

But he manages to find "a bit of blue sky" where others
can see only dark clouds. He finds evidence of hope in the
threatening words quoted from the song of Moses: "I will
provoke you to jealousy with that which is no nation."[1] And
he backs up his "God forbid", by the remark: "but by their
fall salvation is come to the Gentiles, for to provoke them to
jealousy."[2] This may be paraphrased as follows: "The facts
do not mean final rejection. The construction which I put on
them, in view of Moses' words, is this: that which has been the
cause of making the Jews stumble, Jesus Christ crucified, has
as we know, brought salvation to the Gentiles, and this very
salvation has come to the Gentiles in order to make the Jews
feel envious at the loss of privileges which are now enjoyed by
others, and to inspire them to make the effort to recover them for
themselves." This is an ingenious turn of thought; but, for Paul,
it is more than that—it was a deep conviction firmly rooted in
his mind and influencing his whole conduct. For even when
he was busy evangelizing the Gentiles, he had his countrymen
in mind, hoping to reach them in a round-about way through
the conversion of the pagan people to the Christian faith.
When he turned his back upon the Jewish synagogue, and
preached to the Gentiles, this rather suggests that he was
giving up the Jews in despair and that he was not going to
trouble himself about them any more. But it was not so. He
was only changing his tactics. Having failed to win the Jews

[1] Rom. 10.19.   [2] Rom. 11.11.

by the direct preaching of the gospel, he tries to *spite* them into the faith. "Inasmuch then as I am an apostle of Gentiles, I glorify my ministry: if by any means I may *provoke* to jealousy them that are my flesh, and may save some of them."[1] That is, he does his best to convert the non-elect peoples so that the elect people may be made jealous, and at length accept the grace of God in the gospel which they had hitherto despised.

This means that the phrase is something more than an idea introduced into his argument "under the stress of his present train of thought".[2] It is one of the reasons for his zeal in preaching the gospel to the Gentiles. Was he then a great optimist in imagining that if the Jews were made jealous by the conversion of the Gentiles they would eventually see the error of their ways and acknowledge Jesus as the Messiah and so be restored to their rightful place within the commonwealth of Israel? There are some who think so, and it is difficult to give any historical justification for such a hope. The fact is that the Christian Church by its attitude towards the Jewish people has only stiffened Jewish resistance and roused the hatred of Christianity.[3] Yet it is possible that here we have an echo of Paul's own experience in conversion. Paul himself had been roused to anger against the Christians. He was provoked to persecute the members of the early Church because he felt that they were completely wrong in claiming that Jesus was the Messiah. They were, after all, a group of people on the fringe of the law, so how could they be right and the Jews wrong? To believe that God's anointed had come to these people and had been accepted by them was an insult to the God of Sinai. It was blasphemy. So Paul was roused in indignation against them. But it may well have been that such "righteous" indignation was shot through with jealousy. He marked the manner of their life: their steadfastness

[1] Rom. 11.13,14.

[2] C. H. Dodd, *The Epistle to the Romans*, p. 177.

[3] See J. W. Parkes, *The Conflict of the Church and the Synagogue* (1934), and Lukyn Williams, *Adversus Judaeos* (1935).

under torture; the joy and sense of freedom which was apparent even when they were cast into prison or under examination. These people seemed to possess a peace which passed his comprehension at the time, and to which he himself testified when he became a Christian (Phil. 4.7). It would be true to human nature if the fierceness of Paul's persecution of the infant Church was provoked by such jealousy. This was something he could never forget. And because his conversion happened when these feelings of jealousy were at their height, he may have been led to think that a similar conversion would be effected among the Jews if they too could be provoked to jealousy by the very success of his preaching. Whether this was the source of his remark that he worked so hard in the conversion of the Gentiles that he might make the Jews jealous and so move them to accept Christ and share in his riches, we do not know. Nor do we know if any Jew has ever been converted because of being provoked to jealousy. But it is certain that there are those who have come into the Christian Church because they have seen in the gospel the fulfilment of the message spoken by the prophets. They have been provoked by the truth of the Christian claim that Jesus is the Messiah, they have been stimulated into action by this and grafted into the vine through baptism.

In like manner Paul may have hoped that if his preaching to the Gentiles was successful and they manifestly enjoyed the blessings of the gospel, the Jews too would be provoked into action, first perhaps in opposition, but later in acceptance. Such was Paul's *modus operandi*, and such was his motive; and he expected the Gentile readers to sympathize with him both in motive and method. They will lose nothing, he assures them, by such generous conduct. If they have benefited by the failures of the Jews, they will benefit more by their rising again. The ultimate union of Jew and Gentile in the Body of Christ will bring blessings to themselves and to a world long cursed with divisions between man and man and race and race. It will be the fulfilment of God's purpose for mankind.

THE MEANING OF ELECTION

This tremendous conception, that the rejection of the Jews in favour of the Gentiles was not an absolute rejection, but a new way of creating unity in the world is not only an example of the invincible optimism of Paul. It also throws light upon Paul's way of thinking about *election*. These chapters in the Epistle to the Romans have been used by theologians and others in entirely wrong ways. They are not a contribution to the doctrine of eternal predestination of individuals to everlasting life or death. Their theme is not the election of individuals but of a people. Paul is thinking of election in terms of God's choice of men in community to peculiar conditions of privilege and responsibility. The Jews were, in the words of Athanasius, "the sacred school of knowledge of God and of the spiritual life to all nations". When they converted the trust committed to them into an occasion of boasting and an irresponsible prerogative right in God's favour, they became an obstacle in God's way, instead of an instrument in his hands for the blessing of all people. They were as a people temporarily disinherited, and the promises limited to the Remnant which was at one time reduced to one person, Jesus Christ, and subsequently grew in numbers as more people, Gentiles and Jews, were attracted into the Church. The rejection of the Chosen People of the Old Testament was only a stage in the process of God's education, in order to reduce them to that state of humility in which again, in company with "their sisters Sodom and Samaria"[1] they might be grateful recipients of the divine compassion on the basis of faith.

Before passing from this topic it may be worth while to note the kind of analogies used by the Apostle to denote the function

[1] Ezek. 16.44–63.

of the elect in the world. Whereas our Lord employed for this purpose the analogies of light, salt, and leaven, Paul speaks of the firstfruits of a harvest presented to God and so sanctifying the whole crop, and of the root of a tree, the goodness of which determines the character of the branches and of its produce.[1] The former analogy emphasizes the representative character of the elect. There were ten men in Sodom whose presence saved the whole community. The latter analogy points to the vital influence of the elect in society. They are the branches of a tree from the root of which rises up through trunk and branches a spiritual sap which is ultimately transmuted into Christian virtues and actions.

The Apostle, then, expresses his belief that Israel will at length be provoked to jealousy, in other words, that the now unbelieving Chosen People will one day be converted to Christianity. This optimistic thought occupies the remainder of chapter 11. Here he has recourse to the metaphor of grafting. What has happened, he says, is that some branches of an olive tree have been broken off, and a wild olive slip, the Gentile Church, has been grafted into their place. The branches were broken off for unbelief, but it is hoped that their unbelief will not be final, that on the contrary the several branches will again be grafted onto the tree.[2]

Paul is sometimes criticized in the use of this analogy by those who completely misunderstand what he has in mind. It is said that he comes far behind our Lord whose utterances were always true to nature. The process of grafting a wild slip on a good olive is bad horticulture, and the process of regrafting broken-off branches is impossible. The whole point of Paul's argument is that the process is an unnatural one. He is thinking not in terms of nature but of grace. Against the nature of both the wild and the cultivated olive the Gentiles

[1] Rom. 11.16.
[2] Rom. 11.17–23. Hosea and Jeremiah had likened Israel to an olive tree, Hos. 14.8; Jer. 11.16.

have been saved. A new creation has taken place. The major miracle is the acceptance of the Gentiles, the minor miracle is the return of the Jews. An important part of the analogy lies in the fact that the tree remains, though the worthless branches are lopped off. In the words of Christ recorded by the Fourth Evangelist,[1] he is the True Vine and "every branch in me that beareth not fruit, he taketh it away". Israel is the tree, though in the time of Christ he alone was Israel, the faithless Jews had been cut off from the vine, and others had been pruned by the Husbandman that they might bear more fruit. But nothing is said of the return of the branches which had fallen to the ground. Paul includes in his analogy both the ingrafting of the Gentiles and the grafting back again of the natural branches. According to Paul, the Christian Church had its roots in the Old Testament. Although the natural branches had failed the root remains. The root is the Messiah who is identified with the true Israel. It is into this root that the Gentiles are grafted when they are incorporated into Christ through baptism.[2] The Christian Church is not something new, it is as eternal as Christ in whom God has chosen us before the foundation of the world.[3] Paul, however, warns the Gentiles that the same thing can happen to them as happened to the Jews. "For if God spared not the natural branches, neither will he spare thee." This is indeed a warning to Christians of every generation. Though the Church itself, the Root, the Vine, cannot be destroyed, the faithless members may come under the judgement of God and be cut off. This may apply to groups of Christians, to "churches", as well as to individuals. But Paul's final word is one of ultimate hope for God has the power to graft them in again.

[1] John 15.2.
[2] See J. Jocz, *A Theology of Election* (1958), pp. 114 ff. Barrett in his commentary identifies ῥίζα of Rom. 11.16 with the Jewish Christians, who now represent the Remnant, p. 216.
[3] Eph. 1.4.

CONCLUSION

It is well to note in conclusion the relativity of many of Paul's utterances, and the necessity of balancing one statement with another. In this case Paul speaks of the "severity" of God,[1] the literal meaning of which is the habit of pruning or lopping off the faithless members of his Church. But later on in the same chapter he ascribes to God exactly the opposite quality, the habit of restoring privileges which had been forfeited through sin when men abandon their unbelief and turn to him in faith and love. God's dealings with men are not determined by mechanical and unalterable decrees. God's will is neither arbitrary nor capricious, it is the expression of his faithfulness which causes him to punish or to forgive. Paul sometimes makes no attempt to reconcile such antinomies as the goodness and the severity of God. But in this instance he does offer a solution. It is to treat the pruning, the cutting off, or to revert to an earlier expression of his, the blinding, or hardening, as conditional upon the state of Israel's soul. "All Israel shall be saved",[2] he boldly proclaims. The mystery of the past shall be matched by a mystery to be revealed in the future. The mystery of the past, hid *in* God, not from him, was the admission of the outside nations to participation in the Messianic salvation. That mystery has now been revealed and is a mystery no longer.[3]

The other mystery, the mystery of the future, is the ultimate softening of Israel's heart, so that she too will take her rightful place in the one grand fellowship of faith and hope and worship. Paul expects this because Israel is God's child and the object of God's love, "they are loved for the Father's sake".[4] As the Gentiles have benefited from Israel's unbelief, so it is right that the Jews should benefit from the mercy shown to the Gentiles and at length share it with them. So in

---

[1] Rom. 11.22.   [2] Rom. 11.26.   [3] Cf. Eph. 3.4.
[4] Rom. 11.28.

the end the righteousness of God will be vindicated: all alike *may*[1] become partakers of the divine mercy; there is no room here for envy, only the lifting up of the heart in praise to God.

It is fitting, therefore, that as Paul comes to the end of this theological exposition of the ways of God, argument should give place to worship and apologetic to wonder at the inscrutable wisdom of God. "O the depth of the riches both of the wisdom and the knowledge of God: how unsearchable are his judgements and his ways past finding out: For who hath known the mind of the Lord? or who hath been his counsellor? or who hath first given to him, and it shall be recompensed unto him again? For of him, and through him and unto him, are all things. To him be the glory for ever. Amen."

[1] There is no certainty. To say *Dieu pardonnera: c'est son metier* is a blasphemous presumption. See E. Brunner, *The Christian Doctrine of God* (1949), p. 334.

BIBLIOGRAPHY

Angus, S. *The Mystery Religions and Christianity*, 1925
Barrett, C. K. *A Commentary on the Epistle to the Romans*, 1957
—— *New Testament Essays: Studies in the Memory of T. W. Manson* (ed. Higgins), 1959
Barth, K. *The Epistle to the Romans*, 1933
—— *Christ and Adam*, 1956
—— *A Shorter Commentary on Romans*, 1959
—— *The Teaching of the Church Regarding Baptism*, 1954
Best, E. *One Body in Christ*, 1955
Bevan, E. *Hellenism and Christianity*, 1921
Bousset, W. *Kyrios Christos*, 2nd ed., 1921
Brandon, S. G. F. *The Fall of Jerusalem and the Christian Church*, 2nd ed., 1957
Brunner, E. *The Letter to the Romans*, 1959
Bultmann, R. *Essays, Philosophical and Theological*, 1955
—— *Primitive Christianity in its Contemporary Setting*, 1956
—— *The Theology of the New Testament*, 2 vols., 1952
—— *Faith* (Bible Key Words), 1960
Caird, C. G. *Principalities and Powers: A Study in Pauline Theology*, 1956
Cave, S. *The Gospel of St Paul*, 1929
Cullmann, O. *Baptism in the New Testament*, 1950
Daube, D. *The New Testament and Rabbinic Judaism*, 1955
Davies, W. D. *Paul and Rabbinic Judaism*, 2nd ed., 1955
Deissmann, G. A. *Paul, A Study in Social and Religious History*, 1926
Denney, J. *The Death of Christ* (ed. Tasker), 1950
Dibelius, M. and Kümmel, W. G. *Paul*, 1953
Dodd, C. H. *The Epistle to the Romans*, 1932
—— *The Bible and the Greeks*, 1935
—— *Journal of Theological Studies*, xxxii
—— *The Meaning of Paul for Today*, 1922
Edersheim, A. *The Life and Times of Jesus the Messiah*, 1906

Flemington, W. F. *The New Testament Doctrine of Baptism*, 1948
Foerster, W. *Lord* (Bible Key Words), 1958
Fridrichsen, A. (ed.), *The Root of the Vine*, 1953
Fuller, R. H. *The Mission and Achievement of Jesus*, 1954
Goguel, M. *The Birth of Christianity*, 1953
Gore, C. *St Paul's Epistle to the Romans*, 1907
Halliday, W. R. *The Pagan Background of Early Christianity*, 1925
Hanson, A. T. *The Wrath of the Lamb*, 1957
Hooker, M. D. *Jesus and the Servant*, 1959
Hoyle, R. B. *The Holy Spirit in St Paul*, 1918
Hunter, A. M. *Paul and His Predecessors*, 1940
—— *Interpreting Paul's Gospel*, 1954
Jackson, F. J. and Lake, K. *The Beginnings of Christianity*, 1920–35
Jocz, J. *A Theology of Election*, 1958
Johnson, A. R. *The One and the Many in the Israelite Conception of God*, 1942
Johnston, G. *The Doctrine of the Church in the New Testament*, 1943
Kennedy, H. A. A. *St Paul and the Mystery Religions*, 1913
—— *The Theology of the Epistles*, 1948
Kirk, K. E. *Romans* (Clarendon Bible), 1937
Kittel, G. (ed.), *Theologisches Wörterbuch zum Neuen Testament*, vi volumes
Klausner, J. *From Jesus to Paul*, 1944
Knox, W. *St Paul and the Church of Jerusalem*, 1925
—— *St Paul and the Church of the Gentiles*, 1939
Kraeling, C. H. *Anthropos and Son of Man*, 1927
Kümmel, W. G. *Promise and Fulfilment*, 1957
Lake, K. *The Earlier Epistles of St Paul*, 1911
—— *Paul: His Heritage and Legacy*, 1934
Lampe, G. W. H. *The Seal of the Spirit*, 1951
Lee, E. K. *The Religious Thought of St John*, 1950
—— " Unity in Israel and Unity in Christ " in *Studies in Ephesians* (ed. Cross), 1956
—— *The Meaning of Salvation*, 1959
Leenhardt, F. J. *The Epistle to the Romans*, 1961
McNeile, A. H. *New Testament Teaching in the Light of St Paul's*, 1923
—— *St Paul*, 1932
—— *An Introduction to the Study of the New Testament*, rev. ed., 1953
Manson, T. W. *Bulletin of the Ryland Library*, 1948
Manson, W. *Jesus the Messiah*, 1943

Moffatt, J. "Righteousness" in Hastings' *Dictionary of the Apostolic Church*
—— *Grace in the New Testament*, 1931
—— *Love in the New Testament*, 1929
—— *An Introduction to the Literature of the New Testament*, new ed., 1949
Montefiore, C. G. *Judaism and St Paul*, 1914
Moore, G. F. *Judaism in the First Centuries of the Christian Era*, new ed., 1950
Moule, C. F. D. *An Idiom Book of New Testament Greek*, 1953
Moulton, J. H. and Milligan, G. *The Vocabulary of the Greek Testament*, 1930
Munck, J. *Paul and the Salvation of Mankind*, 1959
Nygren, A. *A Commentary on Romans*, 1952
Parkes, J. W. *Jesus, Paul and the Jews*, 1936
—— *The Conflict of the Church and the Synagogue*, 1934
Pierce, C. A. *Conscience in the New Testament*, 1955
Prat, F. *The Theology of St Paul*, new ed., 1957
Rashdall, H. *The Idea of the Atonement*, 1920
Richardson, A. *An Introduction to the Theology of the New Testament*, 1958
Robinson, H. W. *Redemption and Revelation*, 1942
—— *Law and Religion* (ed. Rosenthal), 1938
Robinson, J. A. T. *The Body of Christ*, 1952
Robinson, J. M. *The Problem of History in Mark*, 1957
Sanday, W. and Headlam, A. C. *Romans*, 1920
Schlatter, A. *The Church in the New Testament Period*, 1955
Schoeps, H. J. *Paul*, 1961
Schrenk, G. *Righteousness* (Bible Key Words), 1951
Schweitzer, A. *The Mysticism of Paul the Apostle*, 2nd ed., 1953
—— *Paul and His Interpreters*, 1948
Scott, C. A. A. *Christianity according to St Paul*, 1927
Stacey, W. D. *The Pauline View of Man*, 1956
Stauffer, E. *New Testament Theology*, 1955
Storr, V. *The Problem of the Cross*, 1919
Taylor, V. *The Gospel according to St Mark*, 1953
Thornton, L. S. *The Common Life in the Body of Christ*, 1946
Williams, Lukyn. *Adversus Judaeos*, 1935
Zuntz, G. *The Text of the Epistles: A Disquisition upon the Corpus Paulinum*, 1946

INDEX

Date Due

JAN 17 72	MAY 2 '84		
Oct 26	MAY 11 '84		
FEB 24 72			
MAR 8 72			
OCT 18 72			
NOV 10 72			
NOV 28 72			
DEC 13 72			
OCT 27 73			
SEP 11 '73			
DEC 27 74			
DEC 8 '74			
DEC 18 74			
MAR 2 77			
SEP 26 78			
DEC 13 '78			
JAN 23 '79			